UNCERTAIN LIVES

Children of Promise, Teachers of Hope

UNCERTAIN LIVES

Children of Promise, Teachers of Hope

ROBERT V. BULLOUGH Jr.
Foreword by Nel Noddings

Teachers College, Columbia University
New York and London

Published by Teachers College Press, 1234 Amsterdam Avenue, New York, NY 10027

Library of Congress Cataloging-in-Publication Data

Bullough, Robert V., 1949–
    Uncertain lives : children of promise, teachers of hope / Robert V. Bullough, Jr. ;   foreword by Nel Noddings.
        p. cm.
    Includes bibliographical references (p.   ) and index.
    ISBN 0-8077-4046-2 (cloth : alk. paper)—ISBN 0-8077-4045-4 (pbk. : alk. paper)
        1. Poor children—Education (Elementary)—United States—Case studies.
    2. Poor children—United States—Social conditions—Case studies.
    3. Socially handicapped children—Education (Elementary)—United States—Case studies.   I. Title.
    LC4091 .B85   2001
    372.18'26942—dc21   00-066671

ISBN 0-8077-4045-4 (paper)
ISBN 0-8077-4046-2 (cloth)

Printed on acid-free paper
Manufactured in the United States of America

08   07   06   05   04   03   02   01   8   7   6   5   4   3   2   1

FOR THE CHILDREN

Contents

Foreword

What can schools do when children suffer poverty, poor parenting, bereavement, violence, or disruptive transience? Robert Bullough tells a powerful story here of how good-hearted elementary school teachers work to overcome such problems. But even near-heroic efforts are often not enough. One's heart aches on reading these stories from "the other side of the teacher's desk."

I came away from this book angry—angry with a government that allows so many children to live in poverty, and angry, too, with well-intentioned educators who insist that "poor children can learn as well as rich children." They cannot. I do not mean to suggest that poor children are inherently less capable than their well-to-do peers. I mean simply that family resources matter, that important educational resources we take for granted in middle-class homes are lacking for these children. Further, poverty carries with it a complex package of other ills that make learning difficult.

Toward the end of his book, Bullough says straight out, "Hundreds of thousands of children—probably millions—have been born to lousy parents: drugged, lazy, uneducated, bitter, slovenly, indifferent, dishonest, disengaged, selfish." But Bullough will not permit us to escape responsibility by affixing one of these labels to an inadequate parent. Many failing parents could be helped; many want help. However, while a parent remains inadequate, children need help from outside, and schools cannot provide everything that is needed.

In several of the cases Bullough discusses, grandparents are doing the hands-on work of parenting. This is a story we hear often, but it gives rise to a paradox. How is it that grandparents can act as loving and effective parents to grandchildren when their own children have turned out so badly? Will today's bad parents turn into good grandparents? I don't know the answer to this, but research may shed some light on the question.

Bullough and the elementary school teachers he describes worry about what will happen to these children once they reach junior high school. Now, at least, they have one caring and competent adult in their lives—one who watches over them all day for a school year. What will happen in the fractured environment of junior high? The prognosis is not favorable, and it underscores a recommendation that many of us are now making: Teachers and students should stay together for several years (by mutual consent, of course) so that caring relations can be established and maintained, and we should work to establish smaller classes and schools.

Even with loving, considerate teachers, several of these children are getting the wrong idea about "caring." They have begun to equate it with strict discipline and coercion. To be sure, these kids *need* fair discipline and structure, but coercion should not be seen as synonymous with care. Bullough notes that the teachers in this study avoided the "pedagogy of poverty." Readers may not be entirely convinced. There is considerable emphasis on homework, rules, duty, and guilt, and there is little discussion of homework specially tailored to make sense to particular students. However, Bullough lived with these people and I trust his judgment; the whole story can never be told in one short book. Still, I urge readers to watch for signs of such pedagogy. Poverty may press teachers into less than desirable forms of pedagogy, just as it presses children into an undesirable role as pupils. The best answer, of course, is to get rid of poverty. Until that is accomplished, teachers must help students not only to learn their school subjects, but perhaps more important, learn what it means to be cared for.

Nel Noddings

Preface

Headlines of horrendous acts committed by young people greet newspaper readers almost daily. Lead stories on the nightly news, complete with graphic pictures, seem to suggest that children are to be feared, schools are dangerous places, and teachers cannot be trusted. These headlines and stories present an image of America that is almost as troubling as the reality of the lives lived by some children. One begins to think that for Americans only bad news is good news. But the real story of America's children, the one that rarely makes the headlines, is more complicated and simultaneously more heroic and more troubling than the one usually told. It is a story that does not fit into sound bites and is not easily captured in a single photograph. It does not seem dramatic, but it is. It is a story of children doing the best they know how under trying life circumstances, and of adults possessing varying degrees of understanding and ability who seek to support them in their efforts. It is the story, or rather stories, of 34 children who attend Lafayette Elementary School that will be told here in *Uncertain Lives*, representative of millions more like them.

Uncertain Lives is written for readers who are concerned with the plight of children and who want to help them. It was also written for elementary teacher education students who soon will be serving America's children, and whose lives will become inextricably intertwined with their lives. The intention is to get underneath the stereotypes of "at-risk" children and the adults in their lives by describing the variety and complexity of their situations, and to put a human and ultimately hopeful face on what are otherwise grim statistics. The labels used so easily and dismissively by many adults to characterize young people will not be used here. The shorthand of labeling makes it easy to ignore a child's experience and uniqueness. In *Uncertain Lives*, the children mostly speak for themselves.

Like many of their peers, the 34 children who attend Lafayette face terrific challenges, yet many of them are doing well in school. All hold promise—every one—and all badly want to do well in school and want to be admired and respected by other children and by adults. Those who are doing well in school are doing so for a variety of reasons; from them much can be learned of value to adults who care about the future. Some of the children are fortunate because grandparents have gotten positively involved in their lives. Teachers also care. Several of the children demonstrate remarkable courage and portray personal characteristics that are inspiring. Each child needs a great deal of help, however, and this assistance is not always forthcoming despite teachers' best efforts. America has an obligation to make certain such help is available; that social, cultural, and institutional conditions exist that will maximize every child's potential to live a safe, interesting, productive, and growth-enhancing life. This, ultimately, is the American dream and promise. In seeking to fulfill their part of this monumental responsibility, teachers face a daunting challenge: They must remain ever faithful and resist the temptation to allow the inevitable disappointment that comes with teaching, especially teaching children whose lives are often harsh and heavy, to slip into unrecognized cynicism. Cynicism increasingly infests the American conversation about children, particularly with regard to poor urban children. To lose faith is to join those other Americans who live in gated and guarded communities. There is no higher moral challenge than to hold on to the promise and goodness of a child when others, even the child, do not recognize that promise, and to see the potential that awaits awakening that lies beneath the labels.

Uncertain Lives is dedicated to the 34 children I interviewed. To assist them and their teachers, royalties will be donated to Lafayette Elementary School to be used as the teachers see fit.

UNCERTAIN LIVES

Children of Promise,
Teachers of Hope

CHAPTER 1

Life Inside Mrs. Sorensen's Classroom

MRS. SORENSEN'S CLASSROOM

The room is crowded, lively. Filling the middle are three long tables made of desks facing one another, with children sitting on both sides. At the front stands Mrs. Sorensen. A rock. Solid. Immovable. Someone the children know they can count on, a fixed point; a rare creature, an adult who makes and keeps promises. An extension of Mrs. Sorensen's personality, the room is boldly decorated, almost loud, busy, energetic, full. At the back of the room, by the sink and drinking fountain, is a large sign. The phrase "Math in Nature" sits on top of mirror images of these same words. Beneath this sign are bright pictures of shells, flowers, webs, leaves, and beehives, each presenting an intriguing natural geometric formation. "When bubbles occur," the caption to one picture reads, "they always cover the smallest surface area possible and enclose a given amount of space." Math. By the sink are baskets for turning in completed work, a paper cutter, stapler, and stand-up fans. The room gets very hot in the late summer and spring, and fans give a measure of relief, but only a small measure in a room packed with the sweating bodies of active children fresh from the asphalt playground, the smallest in the city. Nearby are three computer stations. Cabinets line the back wall and south wall, the sunny window side of the room. School supplies are piled everywhere—folders, reams of paper, stacks that will gradually shrink as the year progresses. At the beginning of the year the stacks are high, and seeing them brings a feeling of anticipation of activities planned but yet to come. Much to do. Much to do. Stuck between two large stacks of paper at the back of the room are 13 boxes of Kleenex tissues. These, too, will dwindle: stuffy noses, sometimes bloody noses, children's tears.

At the front of the room is a large white board upon which is written the weekly schedule and daily assignments, including assignment due dates. There's also a television, overhead projector, American flag, and a small teacher desk, front and center, one that Mrs. Sorensen occupies frequently when class is in session. Off to one side and facing the windows,

Mrs. Sorensen has another desk upon which sits her telephone. She uses this desk when class is not in session. The difference between sitting at one desk or the other is the difference between being on and off stage.

Signs are everywhere. Aphorisms. "I don't give you grades, YOU earn them." "The secret of getting ahead is getting started." On a corkboard panel between the two banks of windows is a set of character education signs with accompanying pictures. "We care." There is a picture of a tug-of-war, of young people who "pull together." "You care." "I care." "I care rules: 1. We listen to each other. 2. Hands are for helping, not hurting. 3. We use I care language. 4. We care about others' things. 5. We are responsible for what we say and do." "Respect." "Responsibility."

Working with Children

Wednesday morning. The worksheet is linked to *Guests*, the book the class is reading. The children are busily working, some in pairs, many alone, answering questions. Freddy works with a friend, knees on the seats of their desks, bodies pressing together shoulder to shoulder, fannies poking high in the air, heads down in anxious conference. Freddy's face is not the face of a child, but of a small, slightly disheveled bowlegged man. He seldom smiles, but when he does it creeps up on him and overwhelms his face, a face used to other expressions, mostly sadness, sometimes fear. With this friend, he seems happy, content, and not just busy. He seems pleased when Mrs. Sorensen talks to him, and likes and needs her attention, good or bad. Mrs. Sorensen reminds the students that their task is to answer the questions thoughtfully, and in their responses to make certain they attend to "the point of the question . . . Is that not true?," she asks. She offers an example: "What was the basic problem Moss [a character in the book] was facing? Look at pages thirty-five and thirty-six." New to the school, Juan is also busily working. Small, wiry, and intense, Juan, like Freddy and his friend, is in a hurry to finish. At 9:15 they will be leaving class for the resource room where they go each day for special help.

9:10 a.m. Mrs. Sorensen explains to the class how concerned she is that so many of them are not getting their parents to sign their daily planners. The daily planner is a means for helping children know what work they need to do, and a way to communicate with parents. She's irritated and animated; this is serious business. Nevertheless, she makes an offer: "If you want, I'll look at your planner every day with you before you go home [if your parents can't help you]. My son," she reveals, "can't do it without me checking his planner every day, [so I'll be glad to help you]."

Without a reminder, Freddy, Juan, and two other boys leave class for resource. They've been taught when and how to leave, without disruption, and they go gladly. The resource room is a good place, a place where they enjoy success and can make mistakes without fear of censure.

Mrs. Sorensen has the students write in their planners and takes care of some school business, then states, "I need everything off your desks. All you need is a pencil." It's time to write. She reminds the students that they are to write a story, and that their task for the day is to get a topic and begin to produce a rough draft that will be revised. Since the assignment was given the day before, most know what they are to do, and some students, such as Mark, begin working before Mrs. Sorensen is finished speaking.

9:33 a.m. Silence: the children are working at their desks. Mrs. Sorensen writes on the board for review what is included when writing a rough draft. Head resting on his left forearm and with a look of determination, white-knuckled, Chuck presses down hard, very hard, with his pencil on his paper as be begins to write. He pauses in his labors periodically to think, then begins again. Chuck writes haltingly, working a bit like cars lined up to turn left in busy traffic. It's stop and go. Always smartly and cleanly dressed, with carefully combed and neatly parted short hair, Mark is busily, almost furiously, writing. His pencil flies, showing none of the resistance of Chuck's pencil. According to Mrs. Sorensen, Mark's aim is to be done first, always first, never second. Life is a competition won by the swift, if not the sure. For Mark, quality often gives way to the aim of quick completion, to have the weight of yet another task removed from his slender, 11-year-old shoulders, unless Mrs. Sorensen makes him rework an assignment, which she occasionally does. Slowly Brad lifts himself up from his desk and saunters to the front of the room, and stands waiting for a time to interrupt Mrs. Sorensen. "Not now, Brad," she says matter-of-factly, not losing a stroke. Without protest Brad turns and wanders to his seat; Brad knows what he is supposed to be doing—he most always does—but he occasionally likes to have confirmation. A word will do, a hug is better, and the innocence of his cherubic smile and sparkling dark brown eyes invites hugging. Brad is disarmingly charming, and he knows it. Sally, a tiny wisp of a girl, pale, yellow-gray, fragile, rumpled, wearing clothing tired and worn with washing, returns from the office, sits at her desk for a brief moment, and walks to the board where Mrs. Sorensen is still writing. She stands by Mrs. S's front-and-center desk, seemingly deep in thought, and asks a quick question. Mrs. Sorensen turns, looks right at her, responds, then resumes writing. Sally returns to her desk, scuffed and too-large shoes on her seat, knees pulled up to her chest—when properly seated her feet don't touch the floor—and quietly sits staring at the concept map on the board that Mrs. Sorensen used to illustrate how brainstorming works, how ideas flow from and connect with other ideas in organizing for writing. Deep in thought, she gnaws the eraser end of her pencil, twisting it over and over in her mouth, gaze unbroken. Getting up, she slides out of her desk and cautiously returns to Mrs. Sorensen's side, then softly asks if she may change her writing topic. "That's up to you, honey, I can't tell you what to do," Mrs. Sorensen says so the entire class can hear. Apparently there is a lesson in her response that others need. "Okay," Sally says, disappointed but understandingly; it's her problem, she knows, but she wishes it weren't. She begins her own concept maps, trying to find a topic that captures her imagination. Eight minutes have passed; it's now 9:41 a.m., and much remains to be done still. For some children, topics need to be decided. For others first drafts need to be completed. For still others, a first sentence struggles to take form.

Lifting his head, Chuck vigorously rubs his eyes and yawns. No doubt, writing with a pencil 3 inches away from one's face is exhausting. Then again, Chuck often seems tired; his head frequently rests on his arm, eyes closed, teetering on the edge of slumber. He likes to cover his eyes, he says, because it allows him to "play a game." He imagines things, imaginary places: "I've been lots of places." Mark gazes out the window toward a clear, ice-blue sky, perhaps trying to catch an idea. Getting one, he energetically resumes his writing. Pages are filled and quickly flipped over. Taking a break and looking around at his classmates but not seeing them, Brad almost silently sings to himself. Brad appears to be elsewhere, and glad to be there. Using his pencil, he drums a primitive beat. He's reached the point of diminishing returns; Brad is through writing for the day unless Mrs. Sorensen catches him off-task. It's been a long few minutes, too long, and he is increasingly restless. He shifts in his seat. Time to rest. Time for other things. Chuck has given up, too.

Sally checks again with Mrs. Sorensen, who is now at her "on-stage" desk, to see if what she has done is acceptable. Sally knows what Mrs. Sorensen will say, but she has the faint hope that this time Mrs. Sorensen will take the responsibility of deciding for her: "If you think you have enough ideas, Sally," Mrs. Sorensen kindly says, "then start writing your rough draft." Once again, it's Sally's responsibility. It always is with Mrs. Sorensen. Silently Brad is mouthing words to his friend across the room, who mouths a response back. Not a sound is heard from either boy, but sound isn't needed for understanding. Sally works on her draft, and writes in huge letters with fat margins as a way of filling pages. It's an old and honorable ploy, one that I know well, which brings with it a wonderful feeling of having gotten a lot of work done in a short period of time with minimal effort. Too bad it's a ploy that has never proven effective with teachers after the second grade, and even then its success is iffy. This is fifth grade: 10- and 11-year-olds are supposed to know better. Chuck begins chatting with a girl nearby, is caught, and told to put his name on the board, with a warning, "no more talking." Recognizing his sin, he promptly goes to the board and does as he was told without even a hint of protest. His name joins Marcie's. Noticing Brad is off-task, Mrs. Sorensen asks, "Brad, did you take your medicine today?" "Yes." "Then get a grip." He returns to his labors.

Twenty minutes have passed by since writing began. Mrs. Sorensen compliments the class for how wonderful they have been for the "past twenty minutes" and asks, "Is this [assignment] something you can think about tonight?" "Yes," the students chant in response. She passes out paper clips and tells the students to put their work together so they can continue with it tomorrow. As she explains their homework, Freddy and Juan return to class from resource room where they have spent the past minutes on language arts in a small class of eight or nine children with the special education teacher. For most of the day they are in Mrs. Sorensen's classroom. As most of the class exits for recess, Mrs. Sorensen walks to Freddy's side and explains what the class has been doing. "I want you to do well, Freddy," she says. But Freddy tells me later he doesn't expect to do well. "I've never gotten upset when I get an F," he says to me, but he wants to do well for Mrs. Sorensen. Altogether eleven students stay in for recess, including Brad, Sally, Freddy, and Chuck. Mrs. Sorensen sits beside and works with each child, checks each one's paper, and excuses them once they have shown that they have done a sufficient amount for the morning.

Sitting in the back of the room, visitors like me are impressed with how much the children accomplish, with the orderliness of the classroom, and with the powerful influence Mrs. Sorensen has on the children, who mostly seem eager to please and to learn. Mark's hands are constantly waving in the air as he seeks Mrs. Sorensen's attention, hoping to be called upon to answer a question or gain clarification when needed. He's obviously engaged. Eager. Sally interacts a great deal with Mrs. Sorensen; more, she tells me, than any other person in the school, including other children, except her younger brother. Sally relies on her for guidance and direction. Freddy works hard, although frequently ineffectively, and Mrs. Sorensen often meets with him at a table in the back of the room out of the limelight while other children are busy at their desks in order to help him get caught up. He is always a bit behind. Freddy says he respects Mrs. Sorensen. Although Juan often wanders about the room, Mrs. Sorensen keeps careful tabs on his work and monitors his behavior closely.

Despite wandering, he is rarely in trouble as he said he was in his previous school. In spite of often coming to school late, sometimes very late, and of having difficulty staying awake some mornings in class, Chuck does well in Mrs. Sorensen's class. His grades, like Brad's, Mark's, and Sally's, are good, but according to Mrs. Sorensen they could be better. These are bright children, she says, and she likes them. Although not doing as well academically as their four classmates, Freddy and Juan show signs of improvement and Mrs. Sorensen is pleased, generally; but still she worries.

Thinking about Children and Their Lives

At a glance, Mrs. Sorensen's fifth-grade class is a good one, filled with nice, well-behaving children, good students. Good behavior and hard work promise bright futures. But life is never so simple, a promise so profuse. Pleasing appearances tell a timid truth; a closer look is needed, a tougher truth told. When told, the stories of these six children speak volumes about America and American public education. Their stories and those of their schoolmates need to be told and need to be heard. Astonishingly, the major reform efforts aiming to improve American public education pay virtually no attention whatsoever to the well-being of children and to the quality of their lives. This, despite the fact that, as David Popenoe has argued, the "collapse of children's well-being in the United States has reached breathtaking proportions."[1] The statistics quoted throughout the chapters that follow support this conclusion. Currently, educational discourse is dominated by economic interests: the nation's need to remain internationally competitive—expressed in a commitment to generating national performance standards, raising the educational bar, and using standardized test scores as proof of performance. Political interests bent on the destruction of public education in the name of choice, interests grounded in a mystifying faith in the power of markets to produce excellence in all human endeavors, are gaining power. Harvey Cox aptly describes this as a faith in "market theology," a form of mythology.[2] One wonders, who speaks for the children?! Here, they and their parents and guardians speak for themselves.

INTERVIEWING

Mark, Sally, Chuck, Freddy, Brad, and Juan were part of the group of children I interviewed from Lafayette Elementary School. They and other children in the school were chosen to be interviewed because, according to their teachers, their lives were more complicated and their living conditions more challenging than other children's lives. Their teachers, including Mrs. Sorensen, were concerned about them.[3] An effort was made to identify children from each of six classes in Lafayette, first through sixth grade, in about equal numbers who were doing well or poorly in school. Many of the children were doing wonderfully well in school and performing at high levels, a fact that is simply awe-inspiring. No other criteria were used for identification.

The children represent a very diverse group. About 30 percent of the school is composed of one or another ethnic minority, including a large contingent of Native American children. These children, who are often poor, trace their ancestries to many parts of the world, from Africa and Bosnia to Persia, South America, and Tonga. About one fourth of each of six classes was interviewed, which required getting student and guardian permission, and each class was observed several times. I became a familiar face, as did a few children I got to know well. Sometimes I read with them, or we interacted in other ways. With some I became a friend. While in Lafayette and during the interviews, I carefully sought to avoid using the children in any way or manipulating them for purposes of data gathering. I sought to be especially sensitive to not press them to respond to my questioning when they clearly did not want to. I was also careful to avoid putting words into their mouths during our interviews or to set an expectation that they needed to say something in order to please me. These are real dangers when working with children, ones that require the greatest care. Based upon the warm reception I continued to receive, even hugs, from the children after interviewing was completed, I believe I was successful maintaining their trust and demonstrating my respect for them. Almost all seemed very happy to have participated.

Getting permission to conduct the interviews proved very difficult with some children, and several children or guardians refused. A refusal had little if any effect on my relationship with the children other than that we didn't conduct a formal interview. After receiving a refusal from a guardian, either verbally or a sentence written on the permission slip sealed in the envelope I sent home with the child, I thanked the child and explained that I certainly understood why parents would feel a little uncomfortable when a strange adult asks to conduct an interview with their child. I gave them a package of Skittles candies to thank them, said everything was all right, and then made certain later to interact as I had before. This is important because children generally do not want to disappoint adults. All told, interviews with 34 children were conducted, recorded, and transcribed. Many of the guardians were rightly suspicious of me but once I explained what I was doing and why, they spoke frankly and openly, as did most of the children. Suspicions softened once it was understood that a book would result from the interviews and my observations which would hopefully be useful to teachers and others interested in children to become more knowledgeable about and sensitive to their life circumstances; and that royalties from the book would go to help support programs at Lafayette. Seven teachers and 17 guardians were interviewed. Among other aims, the caregiver interviews allowed me to verify some of the comments made by the children that strained credibility. In only one instance did I discover that a child fabricated an important story, but his fabrication was more revealing and informative about the child's life than the correction made by his grandmother and by his teacher. Of course, there may have been other fabrications; I was unable to interview every child's guardian to confirm what was said, but I was able to speak with all the teachers who knew the children and often the families in intimate ways. This said, I made it clear to the teachers that I was not asking them to betray any confidences, that I understood some things were off the table for discussion. This was especially important when speaking with the special educator who had access to a variety of confidential materials, none of which became the subject of our conversations.

All names are fictitious, although the names chosen are meant to suggest each child's ethnicity. According to the criterion used, easily half of the student body would have qualified for interviewing. Given current demographic trends, the school, located in the Salt Lake Valley, is becoming like many other urban schools in this nation that have high student turnover and high poverty rates; 45 percent of the children qualify for free or reduced-price lunch, and the percentage is increasing. Poverty rates are growing. Located between the inner city and an old section of town that is gentrifying, as well as near clusters of businesses and older apartment buildings, the area surrounding Lafayette is changing rapidly, simultaneously becoming richer and much, much poorer. As property values have soared, families with children have left the area in favor of larger but less expensive homes in more stable and economically and socially homogeneous suburbs. The older and often run-down apartment buildings and houses converted into rental units in the area have been joined by a residential drug treatment facility, new public housing in renovated apartment buildings, a residential battered women's shelter, a "transitional" apartment building for women and children from a homeless shelter, and a second battered women's shelter where women can stay rent-free for up to 2 years. Given shifting demographics, there is some parental concern that the school will eventually be closed.

CHAPTER ORGANIZATION

In the chapters that follow we will learn more about the six children from Mrs. Sorensen's class and other children attending Lafayette who are bound together by their life circumstances and dreams for the future. I struggled with how to make sense of what the children said and of how best to present it. After multiple readings of the transcripts, however, a set of themes emerged, "recurring regularities."[4] These might be best thought of as plot elements in the life stories of the children. The themes, beginning with their expression in the lives of the six children in Mrs. Sorensen's class, are used to focus and organize all but the last two chapters.

Six themes emerged that profoundly affect how the children go about realizing three basic and universal human aims: establishing identity, finding place and belonging, and gaining control—which calls for competence—over one's life. These aims are embedded in the ongoing struggle of humans to resolve a fundamental paradox, to simultaneously achieve integration and inclusion and differentiation and independence.[5] The challenge of establishing a measure of control over life is a central struggle for most of the children, and an issue that cuts across each chapter. The chapter themes include: (1) poverty; (2) missing fathers; (3) parental drug usage; (4) abuse; (5) injury and death; and (6) family instability. I debated whether or not to include a separate chapter on family instability since this theme runs through each of the others and appears to be an effect whereas the others seem to be causal. This chapter was included, finally, because I realized it could not be excluded, so powerful was the influence of family instability on the children's lives.

Chapters 2 through 7 are meant to stand alone. To minimize the difficulty of managing so many names, very few children will be mentioned in multiple chapters, excluding chapters 8 and 9. In chapter 8 I discuss the children's hopes and dreams for the future (so it will be necessary to revisit children introduced in previous chapters, which may be slightly confusing). In chapter 9 the children's views of schooling are presented and the lives of the children are considered in relationship to educational means that hold promise for helping children at risk. A thematic organization cannot fully represent the issues the children face since they are intertwined, tightly knotted together, and I fear that this decision will underplay their complexity. This complexity is evident in how cause-and-effect relationships are so seldom clear in the lives of the children or, for that matter, in the research literature.[6] For instance, poverty is a factor that influences family break-up, but family break-up powerfully contributes to poverty. Similarly, parental drug use and child neglect and abuse are intertwined. Thus, the thematic divisions are admittedly somewhat artificial since the issues children face come in clusters, not rows. Despite the inevitability of some redundancy, this organization allows highlighting of issues of terrific importance to children and those who care for and about them without, I believe, introducing too much distortion.

Recognizing that the children interviewed represent only 34 families, periodic reference to figures that touch on the wider state of childhood in America is necessary. The statistics used come from a variety of sources, including the Child Welfare League of America—the oldest child advocacy organization in the United States, composed of 900 public and private agencies committed to improving the lives of children and families in crisis and at-risk. Although one might wish otherwise, the figures are not made up; at times they strain even the dark, shadowy side of one's imagination. What they painfully illustrate is that the life experiences of these children are tragically typical of a large and growing portion of children living in America. Finally, an effort is made at the conclusion of each chapter to contextualize the stories and to touch on a range of issues important to teachers and to those who, like them, care about children.

CHAPTER 2

Living in Poverty

To be poor is to not have "enough income to meet basic needs for food, clothing, and shelter."[1] The percentage of children in a school receiving free or reduced-priced lunch is the best available measure of poverty rates within schools. As noted, currently 45 percent of Lafayette children qualify, which is low for an urban school. Nationally, about one in five small children live below the poverty line, and children make up 40 percent of America's poor. Numbers are rising; income disparity and inequality is increasing: The poverty rate for children *increased* 36 percent between 1970 and 1996; it *decreased* during the same period 56 percent for those 65 years and older. Large numbers of children go to bed hungry at night or are at-risk of hunger: 37 percent of all children under age 12 in California, 25 percent in Utah, 39 percent in Louisiana, 27 percent in Ohio, 31 percent in New York.[2] Millions of children are hungry or poorly fed, and often they eat their best meals at school. Grandparents shield some children, a fortunate few. No longer only an urban and rural issue, poverty rates among children are rising rapidly in the suburbs as well. For many children, recently established limits on welfare make the future potentially precarious.

THE CHILDREN

Sally

Sally, who spent so much time seeking Mrs. Sorensen's approval in class, knows want. She wore her best clothes—her pink turtleneck sweater, black skirt, and scuffed, worn, black plastic shoes—to our interview. She'd done her hair up as best as she could. This was an event for both of us. She grinned broadly as we walked toward the library, passed other children, and as I held the door for her to enter the room where we would chat. As though she'd won a sweepstakes prize, she'd announced to several acquaintances that she'd been chosen to be interviewed. She looked forward to the interview. Sally likes attention, but she also likes to talk to adults. When listened to, she is interesting, wonderfully innocent, yet surprisingly worldly and wise.

Sally said that each year she has entered a new school, schools in three different states; she doesn't make friends easily, and each move was painful as she sought to fit in socially and to figure out what was going on in the classroom and what she needed to do to gain the teacher's approval. Despite the difficulty of each move, Sally was pleased to have lived in so many states. Just when Sally begins to feel settled and makes a friend or two, the family moves again, and Sally faces what to her is a horrendous challenge of making her way yet again in a strange place. She tries to be brave, and appears almost grown-up, philosophical about moving, but still she clings to her younger brother, a third-grader—two small children against the world. Sadly, after but 1 year at Lafayette, the family has again moved; and suddenly Sally has yet another "father."

When Sally gets a spare moment she loves to draw, mostly fantasy creatures. "What is your favorite thing to draw?" "A mermaid thing, cuz it's not real—there's no such thing as a mermaid—but I like to draw things that aren't real. Fairy tales. Fairies, monsters." She lights up talking about her creations. But Sally's life is not a fairy tale. With her brother she hurries home from school and, she claims, immediately does her homework, and "I mean *right* after my homework I have to clean up my room and do the dishes for dinner and cook dinner." "You cook dinner? Every day?" Staring straight across the table separating us, and without blinking her blue eyes, Sally responded slightly defensively, "I'm a good cook." "You are?" "What's your specialty?" "I really like tuna casserole and spaghetti with parmesan cheese . . . and mozzarella cheese, too." "Do you make your own sauce?" "No, but I make my own pies. I have a few recipes of my own. . . . One of them is—I made it up—peanut butter and jelly pie." "How do you make that?" "It's really a cupcake kind of thing. I take peanut butter and jelly and put it in a cupcake thing and then, well, first I put bread at the bottom, take the peanut butter and jelly and then place a bread on top and I heat it up, it's really good." "It sounds *good*," I said. "We really like it when the peanut butter melts." She said she began cooking when she was 4 years old. For all the talk about food, Sally's greatest fear is that she will not get enough to eat and will get sick. Who would take care of the family, then? "I worry . . . I [will] end up getting too skinny and die cuz I'm really skinny. I try to keep my health up, but I don't eat that much." I hesitated, not knowing what to say. Health issues are very serious for children in poverty; and poor kids are nearly twice as likely as non-poor children to be in fair or poor health.[3] "Why don't you eat much?" I asked. "I try to eat a lot, but I always have to be served last after dinner, but if there's no food left, I can't eat." "What do you do?" "I go to the store and get me a snack, like an orange or an apple." She counted on breakfast and lunch at school. Sally worries about many things: "I'm kind of a sad person, but I'd like to be happy."

After cooking and cleaning up Sally is exhausted. Her days are long and she falls into bed about 8:30 p.m. Sometimes, if she has the energy, she reads in bed before falling asleep. There are few books in the house, which disappoints Sally, who loves books. But she says she doesn't have much time to read.

Sally's mother has severe diabetes. As I watched her at a distance at the busy café where she works, she moved slowly, deliberately, as though her legs were leaden and getting heavier with each step. Her movements are those of a weary, older woman, not of a young woman, tall, thin, and at one time athletic. "She was a champion [roller] skater," Sally proudly proclaimed. Sally's mother seemed to will herself from table to table. I left the café before she saw me, before she had to will herself across the large room to my table. I felt awkward leaving but could not bear having her wait on me. Once her 10-hour shift is finished, Sally's mother laboriously treads the four blocks to her apartment, collapses on the old sofa in the front room nearest the door, smokes a cigarette or two, and eventually sleeps, exhausted.

Sally's stepfather at the time of our interview was a kind and gentle dreamer. Perpetually starting a new business of one kind or another, he seldom made any money, not even a sufficient amount to fix his badly damaged teeth. He sent Sally around the apartment complex with catalogues hoping she would get their neighbors to purchase something, but to little avail. When he was in the home, Sally shared his dream that one day he would succeed, and a happily-ever-after ending would follow. He gave Sally hope. Sally's mother explained that her husband was of little help around the house, having both "mental and physical problems himself, so there is no help [for Sally] there." A few months later she left him.

Neither parent was involved in Sally's schooling. Parent-teacher conferences were troubling for Sally, who attended them alone and made excuses for her parents. She acted bravely. Prior to the spring conference, Mrs. Sorensen caught me in the school hallway and asked if I would be willing to attend with Sally as a kind of friend and supporter. "Sure," I said, wondering if her parents would object. They did not. Sally liked the idea of me attending the conference as well, and appeared right on time dressed in her finest—the black skirt and pink turtleneck she wore to our interview. She seemed pleased I dressed solemnly as befitting the occasion, wearing a dark dress suit, white shirt, and tie. This was serious business. During the conference, I shared some information about Sally's home life—information Sally simply could not share—that I thought Mrs. Sorensen didn't know and should know since it profoundly affected Sally's school performance. During the conference we three planned together for the future, and Mrs. Sorensen and I praised Sally's accomplishments and expressed our pride in her. Afterwards, I drove Sally and her brother to their apartment; as I drove they chatted noisily, happily, all the way. It had been a very good day for Sally, and it had been a very good day for me. Finally, I had been able to do something for Sally, something that made her smile.

Sally carries a terrific burden for one so small and so very young. Her mother sobbed as she told me that Sally is responsible for the family. "She mutters under her breath a little bit; she doesn't have a lot of freedom." Tears streaming down her face, Sally's mother reached for a tissue, wiped her nose, and explained: Sally has "taken a lot on from an early age. She learned how to cook meals when she was seven. She has helped me with the baby since I brought the baby home. She knew how to feed her, change her, everything. Sally was only six when she was born." Hoping she receives some assistance, I asked, "Does her brother help?" "No. He has got some problems with hyperactivity, so he doesn't obey. I've come to realize that until I can get him some help, it is just the way it is going to be."

Although Sally says that she does her homework as soon as she gets home, often she doesn't. As busy as she is, and despite Mrs. Sorensen's best effort, she tends to forget her homework. Other things occupy her attention, like making dinner.

When she can, Sally sneaks out of the apartment and visits a nearby violin-making shop where one of the employees who has taken a shine to her gives her a free lesson. Sometimes she tells her mother a story, not quite a lie, about the bridge of the violin needing to be fixed, for example, as an excuse to go to her lesson. Sally thinks she is fooling her mother with these stories, but she isn't—her mother knows about the lessons but doesn't want Sally to know she knows. "I know she sneaks over there. I have caught her coming out of there. I darted around the corner so she wouldn't see me. I know she sneaks over there." Sally thinks she has to sneak out or tell a lie to go for a lesson, to do anything that is pleasureful for herself. The school also offers after-school weekly lessons. A broad grin covers Sally's face as she talks about these sanctioned lessons. Why her mother perpetuates the deceit is puzzling, but she does.

Considering the family's situation, and the life of her daughter, Sally's mother seems to shrink into despair as she speaks. Each family move was undertaken with the hope of a better life, but the family's situation has steadily worsened; and each move slices away a bit of what hope for the future remains. In Las Vegas Sally's mother developed a gambling habit, so they fled. She stopped gambling, but given her health problems she could not obtain a job that equaled the pay she received as a card dealer, and had to settle for waitressing at the café I visited. Poverty wages. No benefits. "My greatest fear," she says, "is that the cycle of poverty, and just the hopelessness of life, is [breaking] Sally. I don't want her to have to live like my mother lived, and like I live. I want it better for her. [I want her to have] the opportunity to be and do anything she wants when she gets older." "Do you see some hopeful signs in her, that she can break that cycle?" "Not unless I can find a way, unless she buckles down in school and starts getting good grades so that she can get scholarships to college. I don't see it happening. It just kills me because I know the potential that is there. . . . For three years I have tried to tell her, 'Don't be like me. Don't you be like this for all your life. You don't want [to live like] this. You want something better. You can do and be anything you want to be. You can do anything you want to do if you just apply yourself now. Just put in a little bit of effort now, and later it will make your life so much easier."

Sally appears to understand her mother's message, and wants to believe it. She dreams of being an astronaut, and knows she needs to go to college to have any chance of reaching that goal. "Are you going to go to college?" "I hope so," she said, lowering her head, "but we're so broke I don't think we're going to make it." I hope so, too, that she can someday leave earth for space.

Exhaling smoke, Sally's mother expressed fear that Sally will follow in her footsteps and connect with unreliable men, men like Sally's father who abandoned the family. Speaking rapidly, intensely: "He disappeared into thin air. He just never called, never showed up, just disappeared. I can't find him. I have tried . . . I had a private investigator back home [try to find him]. . . . I can't find him . . . He is apparently either dead or living under an alias and using somebody else's social security number. Or, he is in jail . . . He was a shyster. That is why I threw him out in the first place. He was always scheming. Every job he had he'd get fired for stealing and he'd swear up and down he didn't do it. 'Steal? Me? Never.' I mean, a pattern was developing. I am not stupid." To Tommy, Sally's brother, the father was dead. Subject closed.

Sally thinks she is a good student. Yet she was bothered that Mrs. Sorensen punished her for not getting her parents to sign her daily reading contract. When "you have to read a book to your parents and if they don't listen they're not gonna know what the story's called, so if they can't sign [the contract], you'll have to read it until they listen. That's only how your teacher knows when your parents really listen to you

[read]." Sally's parents didn't sign, and so she lost credit until in our surrogate parent-teacher conference I explained to Mrs. Sorensen what Sally was struggling to do, and an alternative plan was made that allowed Sally to sign her own contract, on her honor. Sally liked the plan, and seemed greatly relieved. She had read *Swiss Family Robinson* and *Black Beauty*; now she would receive credit for reading them. *Black Beauty* thrilled Sally, and her imagination ran wild. She talked excitedly about how her brother agreed to be a horse and had taken her for a ride. Now, she is positive she knows what it must be like to sit atop a sleek steed.

At school, Sally is an outsider. As I witnessed, other children sometimes pick on and tease her, but often she sets up other children so they get into trouble with their teachers because of something she did. She tattles. She cries. But Mrs. Sorensen loves her: "Sally is just a sad little waif in the drop of the sparkling sea. I'd take her home in a second. She is a doll. She is sweet. She wants to please. She is so starved for attention that that is where all her negative comes from because she does stupid things to get attention. She is a hypochondriac. She is very dramatic. You just barely touch her and she needs to go to the hospital. But, she is doing better with that, though. I get less and less of that. . . . She is very smart, too . . . She has no social life. I don't think she knows what it means to go roller blading or roller skating with some girls or to laugh and giggle in a bedroom because they are having a sleep-over. She has missed out on childhood already, and she is only in the fifth grade. . . . The kids make fun of her. Nobody chooses her as a partner ever, they still don't. Sweet things like Heidi and Annie will kindly accept her in a group because I nod to them, and they know they have to and they are not mean about it, they do it. . . . She needs a lot of attention."

Clinton

For those who don't know Clinton's mother, a first meeting is a tad shocking. It was for me. She's "into heavy metal," Mrs. Novakovich, Clinton's teacher, said. Metallica is her favorite group. She's articulate, insightful, and a walking advertisement for body-piercing and tattooing; various bits of shiny metal enter and exit her ears, nose, and eyebrows. She changes her hair color regularly, preferring purple and bright hues of red as complements to black leather clothing. For dress-up occasions such as back-to-school night, which she faithfully attends, she spikes her hair, which delights Clinton, who brought his mother to show-and-tell and proudly introduced her to his obviously interested classmates.

Clinton fancies himself a fashion plate but of a different sort from his mother: soft edges to his mother's hard edges. A tall, heavyset third-grader, Clinton likes frills, brightly colored tennis shoes, trinkets and jewelry, colorful feminine clothing, and wears his luxuriant tinted black hair, which reaches the small of his back, in waves, curls that playfully drape around his chubby round face and cascade over his broad shoulders. He's very particular about his appearance. Clinton gets furious, then cries, when other children ask if he is a girl. It is easy to understand the confusion; their questions are sincere, not spiteful. His friends are girls; he engages passionately in girl games. He is different from the other children, and so they wonder.

Clinton has an older half brother, who, like Clinton, has never known his father, a violent man who has been in federal prison for a decade. Neither man has any involvement with their son, nor do they provide any support, so Clinton's mother has been completely on her own. She admits that her life choices alienated her family, who apparently had great difficulty accepting her having gotten pregnant out-of-wedlock twice by two African-American men; her sons are biracial.

Speaking deliberately, quietly, Clinton's mother expressed some of her concern for him: "There are times when I really enjoy [Clinton's] company, but other times I don't want to be around him because he is screaming, bawling. He has like fits. . . . The boys wanted to watch a movie. I am always making sure, 'Now you know this movie doesn't get over until after nine and you aren't going to watch the end [before having to go to bed], so do you want to watch something else?' 'No, I don't care about the movie I just want to watch a little bit.' Okay, first mistake. So, at nine o'clock it is your bedtime and it is like, 'let me watch one more part.' 'No, it is nine o'clock and bedtime.' Then he screams for forty-five minutes. Forty-five minutes, I'm not kidding. This was just recently. . . . I sat out on the couch with [his brother] waiting for the police to come to the door. . . . Finally [his brother] said, 'Why don't you just go in there and spank him?' I can't. I have to totally pull myself away from him. Boy . . . The next day, the neighbor came over and said, "So, you didn't let Clinton watch any extra television last night.' I was like, 'I'm really sorry.'" At the beginning of the school year, Clinton's mother warns his teachers that he is very sensitive, and cries easily. His teacher describes him as a child who is manipulative, and cries and falls apart to try and get his way. But with Mrs. Novakovich this strategy failed. He could cry, but he wouldn't get his own way. He was a sickly baby, his mother says, and she "babied him, he got his way. . . . He seemed so sick and that was my excuse right off the bat [for babying him]. I can see now that I wasn't right." That, she says, is the reason why he is as he is. Even as some of his behavior concerns her, she adores him, finding him a sensitive, interesting child: "I wouldn't change him."

The boys are Clinton's mother's life. She has been on welfare for several years, and is now facing the possibility that she must get employment, but doing what? She reported having no particular job skills. She stopped working when Clinton was born, and has not had employment since, although she has tended other people's children as a way of supplementing welfare without reporting her income.

The room where we spoke reflected her disposition at the time, dark, closed-in, and depressing. Much was on her mind. An old couch faced a large color television set and a video-game system. On one wall hung a huge Darth Vader poster; shrinelike, pictures of her beloved sons were displayed everywhere. She's "clinically depressed," she said, and has other health problems. She thinks she has learning disabilities but isn't certain because social services will not pay for testing for attention deficit disorders at her age, 34 years old. She doesn't believe she can work; she wishes she could. Besides, the only jobs she might obtain pay little, less than a living wage. Seventy-eight percent of the jobs created in Utah during the 1990s pay less than a living wage, and then she wouldn't be home to help Clinton with his schoolwork, and as she rightfully says, he needs a great deal of help. So the family gets by, but for how much longer? she worries.

Clinton struggles with reading and especially mathematics; even simple addition puzzles him. But because of his mother, his best friend, he does his homework faithfully and he likes to read, even though he is a full grade or perhaps more below level, according to his teacher. Each day he reads with his mother and they talk about what they read. Clinton's mother is a reader, she says, and the proof is that there are lots of books in the small, cluttered apartment. Books are important enough that despite her limited income, she invests in them. She doesn't miss parent-teacher conferences, and is in contact with Clinton's teachers to keep abreast of his performance and to share her concerns. Recognizing that he wanted to do well, and that he usually did his work but wasn't progressing as she hoped, Mrs. Novakovich requested permission from Clinton's mother to have him tested for learning disabilities, but after giving verbal permission, she did not sign a release. Mrs. N. is certain that she will soon.

Stereotypes of welfare mothers aside, Clinton's mother is engaged in his education; and given the difficulties he has in school, one wonders what would happen if his mother wasn't available to assist him. Certainly no one else would step in to fill the void, so he would slip even further behind his classmates. This is the trade-off Clinton's and many other mothers face: To work outside of the home means being less involved in her children's education, both of whom desperately need consistent adult assistance; the work she will probably get is low paying, unlikely to raise their standard of living while perhaps permanently harming her children. She might even lose the family's health benefits. The working poor lack such benefits. In fact, more than 11 million children lack health insurance in America.[4] No wonder she worries.

Rolf

"Rolf is a genius," Brad, from Mrs. Sorensen's room, said, grateful for this good and interesting friend. Brad is probably right. One afternoon Rolf and I read together sitting in the hallway. Rolf is a space buff, hoping, like Sally, to be an astronaut one day, so he chose for us to read an astronomy book. Buzzing along, pronouncing technical terms with ease in his deep small-boy voice, he stopped reading suddenly and proclaimed, "That's wrong." Rolf, age 10, then explained to me the mistake he found in the book, one written by a Ph.D. physicist. Rolf's mind races, skipping quickly from one idea to another, and it is difficult to keep up, but one tries because he is, just as Brad said, interesting. Looking, as his teacher remarks, like a miniature "Gene Wilder" but with a speech impediment, Rolf initially demands but eventually commands attention. For being, as he describes himself, the "runt of the litter," Rolf has a huge personality, piquant, almost too large for such a small form.

Rolf speaks of himself in a matter-of-fact way, not bragging, just facts: "When I was in third grade . . . I was ranked the highest reader. In kindergarten, you know those Bernstein Bear books with those kind of long words? Well, I was reading those in kindergarten." He began talking about a recent pulsar discovery that excited his imagination, and suddenly, like other subatomic particles, he was elsewhere: "Could there be life?" he said to himself, allowing me to listen in. "No, because pulsars give off radiation at a level that would kill anything that resembles—hmm, unless maybe it depended on it, right? To live, right?" As the interview proceeded, Rolf spoke of many things: "Gus Grissom, Edward White the second, and Roger Chafee"; his love of NBA basketball; and his interest in El Niño weather changes, which he's certain cause his frequent illnesses. He stated: "The one in November was a cold virus; then in December it was bronchitis, [I'm] a lucky survivor of the deadly cold, common cold, cured . . . there is a proven cure, something in chicken noodle soup, we may never know." As he spoke he rolled between his two fragile pale white hands a Farmer's Almanac he'd been reading, and sometimes as he spoke he read: "I call that reading and talking at the same time." "You are good at that?" "Right. February . . . temperatures will be for the month of June, 37 degrees in the north and 41.5 in the south, thank-you for your cooperation." Rolf may have come to be interviewed, but he controlled the conversation. I may have asked the questions, but we both knew who was in charge.

To help his concentration, Rolf takes Dexedrine three times a day. Ritalin, the most commonly used drug by children, had no effect.[5] "What does Dexedrine do?" "Takes control of me . . . because of my hyperactivity. . . . It's working for a little bit longer than Ritalin." In class, Rolf's mind often wanders—"rushes" is the better descriptor; off-task. He tackles topics that engage him and ignores the rest.

Despite the pleasure he gets from his school studies, Rolf can't be bothered by homework. His mother can't help him, being overwhelmed with her own physical and psychological problems. But he loves school, everything about it: "I love it!" Spelling. Science. Algebra. But he doesn't like change: He wants and needs predictability both in and out of school. It bothered him, for example, that a new requirement was made that classes sit together in the lunch room, which disrupted his routine and interfered with his visiting friends.

His teachers like Rolf and care about him, he said, and the proof was that he had been chosen to be a "mud puddle in the first-grade play." "What?" I asked in disbelief. I'd never heard of a child being a mud puddle; a tree, perhaps, but not a mud puddle. "That was the best! I was pretty nervous and then when I got to the funny part, the whole school laughed. Then when I got back to day care, my day care [classmates who attended Lafayette], they were going, 'Hey, there is the star.'" Three years after the event, teachers and other students still remember Rolf's mud puddle. I wish I'd been there.

Interviewing Rolf is exhausting but fascinating. Teaching him, for teachers who lack a sense of humor and of wonder, must be doubly exhausting. But if one can laugh, Rolf is a joy, a trying joy, but a joy nonetheless. He's self-assured in an oddly humble way, unassuming, nonjudgmental, and ever provocative. As his teacher said: "He is just about the most bizarre personality I have ever met in my life. . . . I adore him. He is just delightful." Mrs. Wilson has a wonderful dry sense of humor.

Three questions remained to be asked in our interview when Rolf decided to turn the interview into a version of *Jeopardy!*; humming the game show tune, he stopped and introduced me to his imaginary audience: "Here is your host, Mr. Bullough. . . . With three questions left, Rolf, with $10,780 dollars and the others with $1,000 something . . . for a hundred points." "Okay, Rolf, for a hundred points, when something bad happens to you, why does it happen?" "Humm, think, think, think, I'm not sure yet. May be something, humm, humm. Oh, wait! . . . "

The game continued: He let me know that he was well ahead of the other contestants, and in the process went back in time and "saved Kennedy from being shot," a change in history that he said would make him very happy: "That he would go on seeing his dream come true of putting a man on the moon. Even though he didn't get to see that, that dream came true." Suddenly, from being way ahead, "All dollars are tied." Tension builds. I'm imagining the audience with Rolf; they lean forward in their seats in anticipation of Rolf's next answer, perhaps a winner.

I repeat my question; according to the rules, one repetition is allowed: "Rolf, what would make you most happy?" "Think, think, think, before Player B or C gets it. Think, think, think, think, make me most happy." As quickly as he slipped into his contestant role, he slipped out of it: "Life in a house right close to the school. With a backyard that I could actually make a basketball hoop so it doesn't drive my mom crazy, so I can go outside and play. With a patio . . . When you are in an apartment you just don't get to have that much fun." What he didn't say is that there are no children in the area near his apartment—a few upscale condominiums, office buildings, and a gas station are nearby—and he goes crazy being cooped up. It's no fun.

Rolf lives in a tiny, one-bedroom attic apartment, up three tall flights of stairs, in an old converted house. To sit down for the interview with Rolf's mother, clothes and magazines had to be pushed aside on the couch. Nothing is put away; clothes, games, magazines, dishes, videos; stuff is everywhere. The apartment looks a bit like Rolf, at least until my son, Seth, gave him a buzz haircut (at his request and with his mother's permission, of course). "Disheveled" describes Rolf. Several weeks after the interview, Rolf and his sister were taken away from their mother by social services for several days until the home was put in better order. Fretting the entire time, Rolf worried he'd never return. He wasn't alone; about ten children in the school at any one time are either in foster care or under care of social services. Nationally, well over half a million children are in out-of-home care.[6] The mother, a very short roundish and intense woman, tries to organize the apartment but has difficulty doing so. Some days she is unable to get Rolf to the city bus that stops in front of the apartment that he rides to a stop near the school. The family lives just outside of Lafayette boundaries, but Rolf's mother has kept him there to minimize the disruptions in his life. She is aware of his need for order, and does her best to provide it, but struggles, she says.

All three family members are in one kind of therapy or another, together and separately. Rolf's sister, who is brain-injured, disrupts his life and he gets angry, he said, and therapy has helped. He was placed in a social-service-sponsored 3-month behavior modification program that helped him learn "things like personal space, control your anger . . . not arguing, not beating your little bratty sister even though she does sometimes start to fight." Rolf was pleased he'd graduated from the program, at the top of his four-person class: "three people graduated the same day I did," then he named them, and said, "except they were on level four and I was on level five." Not bragging. Just a fact.

A bipolar manic depressive, Rolf's mother receives disability income. She cannot work. His sister receives social security because her injury has produced what her mother describes as a kind of autism. They have little money. According to Rolf's mother, his sister has "really good verbal skills but [is] missing a lot of emotional connections." The father, who Rolf's mother characterizes as abusive and unable to keep a job, left the family when Rolf was 3 and his sister 1 year old. Rolf, she said, didn't begin speaking until he was 3 years old, after the father left. He didn't talk, she thinks, "because he was scared to death to talk. Now that he has started talking we can't get him to shut up. [There were lots of] other problems . . . his sister [was born] four months early. That happened just right when he was turning two and for like six or seven months everything in the whole family focused on her. I feel horrible about it, but at the same time it was one of those things that [had to be done]. I was trying to learn everything that I had to know to [care] for a baby like this when I brought her home. [Rolf's therapy] is aiming to help with his [attention deficit disorder], with problems that he has had with his dad . . . for a time he was very aggressive at home. . . . He'd take and throw things at us. . . . He just gets frustrated with the fact that we don't see the world the way that he sees the world." But who could? "[The therapy is helping]. He has got a good therapist and he meets with her once a week."

When the home becomes unlivable, case workers step in to make certain the apartment is cleaned. Local members of her Mormon congregation reach out to the family, seeking to involve Rolf in scouting and other activities for children, and support the family in other ways, including helping clean the apartment and organize finances. School and a few weeks during the summer with a grandfather in another state are the main sources of stability in Rolf's life. No wonder he doesn't like change at school. Routine is important; predictability for an unpredictable mind.

I've thought a lot about Rolf; it's hard not to. Intellectually gifted, he likely will never be placed in a program for the gifted and talented inside or outside Lafayette; he doesn't fit the required "star profile" for admission, nor does his family fit the family profile. High standardized test scores aside, he's a handful, not an easily controlled, confident, and self-directed achiever that the star profile requires. Nor does he have the high level of parental support demanded. It's a bitter irony. Conformity is part of the institutionalized definition of giftedness. Parental mental illness and poverty as much as his own delightful wackiness put Rolf outside of the definition, to Mrs. Wilson's pleasure. Outside of school, Rolf has few opportunities to develop his talents; stuck in the apartment, he seems to cope by living between his ears.

Randall

When Randall discovered that I was going to interview one of his friends, he sought me out and said that he also wanted to be interviewed. It sounded "fun," he said. But day after day I saw him in school, he'd tell me his mother still had the permission slip but hadn't signed it. Since I knew he badly wanted to be interviewed, I asked if I could drop by his apartment to get the slip. This way, the burden was mine, not his. He liked the plan, and gave me the address. Randall lives in the back portion of a drafty converted trailer sitting on a cinder block foundation and situated in a small parking lot between an older several-story apartment building and a turn-of-the-century house that serves as a real estate office. The front half of the trailer is occupied by a beautician's shop that caters to older women who use copious amounts of hair spray. I know this having spent several hours over a week parked on the street waiting to meet Randall's parents and fearing I would be mistaken by people in the neighborhood as a police officer or social worker. When I heard someone inside the back portion of the trailer, I would knock, but no one would answer. I waited. Late one afternoon I caught Randall's father as he unlocked the door. He froze and peered at me suspiciously as I introduced myself. I explained what I was doing and was told sharply that Randall didn't want to be interviewed. Recalling Randall's enthusiasm, I took courage and assured him that he did, and asked if he would mind asking his son. If Randall didn't want to be interviewed, I said, that would be fine with me. With a wide smile, Randall rushed up to me in the hallway the next day and thrust a rumpled, torn, and mustard-stained but signed permission slip into my hand. He said it had been in the garbage.

A sixth-grade student, Randall has attended seven or eight schools, he said. He came to Lafayette with a reputation as a troublemaker. "He is really a nice kid," his teacher Mr. DeCourse remarked, but he gets into trouble without trying. Trouble dogs him. He hangs out. His parents don't seem to care; he drifts, blown about, almost happily indifferent to events and people surrounding him, completely caught in the moment. Mr. DeCourse related a story: While he and the special education teacher spoke with the parents during a home visit, Randall's older brother was "beating him up in the other room and the parents didn't even care." Listening, Mr. DeCourse didn't know what to do; he was a guest in the trailer. "He's street smart," but doesn't do well in school. In his previous school, children he befriended began missing school, some for a few days. They were found with Randall and his parents where the family was living under a freeway overpass, homeless.

Randall's father does odd jobs and his mother, who has a son living in another state from a previous marriage, gets work where she can, most recently as a store clerk. They move each year, spending summers living in their car and sometimes traveling the Western states and visiting friends. Once cold weather arrives they rent an inexpensive apartment, like their current place which at one time was a brothel. Anticipating warmer weather, they stop paying rent, are evicted, and the cycle begins again. Gypsies, they have few possessions, which include a black-and-white portable television, a radio, an oven missing its door. Randall sometimes sleeps on a pile of laundry. No bed.

Randall doesn't like to read, but he has a favorite book, *Shiloh*. "Tell me about *Shiloh*," I said. "Well, this kid finds a dog and the dog won't quit following him and every time the boy tells the dog to come over he will put his tail between his legs because it ran away from some old guy that used to beat it. He gets to keep the dog." "Why do you like that book?" "It is about life." "Oh," I remarked. "How is it about life?" "Well, how they act and the feelings and stuff." "Is there a character in the book that you really relate to?" "Yeah, the dog." Amazed by what was said, I assumed at first he was teasing me, but his look suggested otherwise: no, he was serious. "Tell me why. That's interesting." "Well," Randall continued, "whenever somebody, well my brother, whenever I will do something wrong he will kick me. So my brother will come and get me in a headlock . . . I kind of flinch [when he's around]." This is what Mr. DeCourse witnessed on the home visit. At times Randall feels like a beaten dog.

In contrast, Randall appreciates how his teachers treat him, which indicates they care for and like him. "How can you tell your teachers care for you, that they like you?" "The way they treat us." "How do they treat you?" "With respect . . . they don't lie to you; [they] tell you their honest opinion." For them, he does some work, sufficient to receive passing grades, but not homework: "[My parents] end up forgetting about me doing my homework and I forget about it, and just leave." In school, Randall is happy, and feels popular and well-liked by other children: "I feel popular. . . . Everybody knows me, they know me as the kid that used to have green hair. . . . The first day here I had green hair."

REFLECTIONS

Randall, like so many of the children interviewed, moved frequently. Poor families often do, ever in quest of affordable housing which is not only difficult to find but even more difficult to keep. Small apartments lend themselves to clutter and disorganization. More than 5 million households in the United States currently either spend over half of their income on rent or live in severely substandard housing.[7] Nice places are rare; there is a serious shortage of public housing. When moves take place during the school year, children miss out on a great deal of instructional time. As rents soar, often there is no choice but to move. Yet even when families move during summer, between school years, children have to reestablish themselves in an unfamiliar context and suffer educationally. Curricula differ, and moves disrupt educational continuity; teachers differ, and new relationships must be forged. It takes time for teachers to understand their students and how best they learn, and many times children are gone before such understanding is gained. These children are forever beginning but never finishing their studies.

Children suffer socially as well. Sally and her small brother cling together. They have no one else. Wherever Randall goes, and the family moves often, he quickly discovers that the most accepting children, the ones most likely to befriend him, are those that themselves are not doing well in school, who share his problems and his worldview. The teachers knew that Alfredo and Randall would quickly find one another, and they did. In one respect, Rolf is very fortunate; his mother has succeeded in keeping him at Lafayette where he is understood, valued, and enjoyed.

Poverty has many causes that interact. The families of these children illustrate but a few: mental illness and poor health; limited education and few skills needed to succeed in an increasingly competitive market; abundant low-income and dead-end jobs but few living-wage jobs; divorce; unfortunate choices. Whatever the sources, poverty negatively affects school performance and hurts children badly. Children in families on welfare are one-third more likely than other children to suffer either serious emotional or behavioral problems and delays in development and growth, or to have learning disabilities. They score lower than better-off children on achievement tests. Analysis of the National Longitudinal Survey of Youth concludes that poor children are more likely to exhibit behavior problems than other children; and children whose families have slipped into poverty exhibit the highest incidence of behavior problems. Poor children are more likely to repeat school grades, be suspended and stop attending.[8] Having escaped poverty, families become more nurturing and stimulating than those that remain on welfare or stay poor. Lacking quality early child care, poor children are more dependent than other children on the public schools to offer them new possibilities for being in and for thinking about the world; skills for gaining understanding and for enriching experience; concepts needed for enhancing meaning; and experiences of wondrous kinds in the arts, sciences, humanities, and on the playground. In school children can dream dreams otherwise deadened by parental poverty. Inner passion can sometimes find expression: a violin for Sally; a library and a basketball court for Rolf.

Lafayette teachers know this, and try to provide such experiences for the children, often spending out of pocket to do so. Each year, for instance, they sponsor a sub-for-Santa program and make certain no child is forgotten. The school is sorely underfunded, however, and there are serious limits to what can be done. Because there is not a sufficient number of children in poverty or judged "at-risk" attending, Lafayette does not qualify for additional district-administered federal funding: Nearly half the student body is not a high enough figure! Pathology and a commitment to remediation rather than prevention guides district administrator reasoning when allocating resources. Robert Slavin and his colleagues at Johns Hopkins University, who have worked extensively with schools to improve the educational opportunities of poor, urban children, put the issue this way: "Despite some improvements and a growing acceptance of the idea that prevention and early intervention are preferable to remediation, the overwhelming emphasis of programs (and funding) for at-risk students remains on remediation."[9] The priorities are simply wrong. Teachers cannot make up the difference between these children's experiences and opportunities and those had by their better-off peers, but they try, and in trying make a positive difference in the lives of the children. So much could be done if Americans thought of each child, especially each poor child, as their own, rather than as someone else's, most especially a teacher's or social worker's problem. It is a hard and dispiriting reality, but public disdain for parents like Randall's often expresses itself in punishment of children in America.

CHAPTER 3

On Men and Fathers

Within Lafayette, about half of all the schoolchildren live with one parent, usually, but not always, the mother. Families are dynamic and changing. Divorce, abandonment, or separation, including when never-married parents split up, were part of the lives of each of the six children from Mrs. Sorensen's class, and of almost all of the children interviewed, some of whom were being reared by grandparents and stepgrandparents, who themselves face unique challenges. Forty-five percent of all children have divorced parents. It is important to recognize that the pressures on single mothers to manage their families alone are immense, and do not decrease as children mature. Sometimes they need special help or accommodation so they can become more involved in their children's education, and teachers need to respond.

Children respond to the absence of a father through divorce or abandonment in diverse and extraordinarily complex ways that play out in their school behavior. Emotions are mixed and frequently confusing to the children, as is their behavior. Anger is common. Daughters tend to "use the mother as an emotional role model" and imitate her anger, while boys often feel sad.[1] The greater the level of the mother's anger, generally the more children act out.[2] A deep sadness often results from children's tendencies to blame themselves when the family breaks up.[3] Academic performance often suffers, even when a family is reconstituted.[4] Hate is the purest emotion, born of rejection, but even it is tinged with longing and love.

ANGER AND DISAPPOINTMENT

"I don't got a dad," Jeri said. Along with being told many good things about her father, Jeri understands that her mother didn't marry him even though he wanted to marry because, as she put it, "he took drugs." Her mother told her so. Lowering her voice, tipping her head to one side and looking longingly away toward the window and playground outside, she said, "He didn't want to be a father anymore." More than this she doesn't know. As she spoke, light seemed to fade from her eyes and she withdrew into herself. Jeri wants to see her father, but cannot. "My mom says that

I can't talk to him, I can't . . . She says I look like him." "You mean, he has beautiful blue eyes, too?" "Yeah, he has blond hair. He is strong like me. My grandma seen him like last year a little bit but she didn't talk to him." A promise that the full story will be told when she is 12 years old proves partially satisfying, but Jeri seems ambivalent: Perhaps the whole story will be painful. She imagines a father—a strong man, a good man, a handsome man; but imagination is a poor substitute for the real thing. "I really want a father, and I want a brother or sister." "I want like a whole family. All my aunts have a husband, but I don't have a dad, and all my aunts' little kids have a dad, and I am the only one that doesn't have a dad." "It hurts, huh?" "Yeah," she said, pausing, but "my uncles are like my dad."

Jeri is an intense, "boy crazy," her mother said, fourth-grader with a quick temper. As I spoke with her mother, who has earned a college degree and is diligently seeking to build a business career to take better care of herself and her daughter, she expressed regret that she didn't marry Jeri's father and now doesn't know where he is, but even as she spoke she quickly qualified her remarks: "He just is not a good father figure, in any stretch." When Jeri needs and wants to talk about her father, her mother brings out a picture she keeps of him and recalls him, fondly remembering him as her "best friend" in high school. When a small child, Jeri assumed her grandfather was her father, which proved confusing as she matured. Fortunately, a large and extended family of aunts and uncles supports Jeri, and is involved every day in her life from an aunt who picks her up at school to uncles who take her on outings with cousins. Jeri knows she is loved, her mother says, but still, as she talks about her life and family there is sadness, disappointment, and more than a touch of anger.

As much as she wants to see her biological father, more than anything Jeri simply wants a dad. She is very clear about that. But she resents her mother dating even as she accepts that her own father is out of the picture.[5] The situation is very complicated, and her mother doesn't quite know what to do: "[Jeri] does not like me going out. She doesn't like to get to know people. She is very possessive of my time. We have been through the whole discussion. . . . I am not going to love you any less. She will always be my number one priority. I mean, we are going on ten years now that we've been a family. She wants instant gratification, but she doesn't want to have to go through the getting to know period and adjustment." From Jeri's perspective, getting her a father shouldn't be difficult, perhaps no more difficult than the effort she made to attract the attention of Calvin, one of the boys in her class: bare midriff, awkward high heels, and, as her teacher said, generally driving "the poor boy crazy." But it is. Her mother dates, but each date comes with a cost, according to her mother: Jeri frets and gets angry; and her mother worries about what Jeri will think of the man she is dating and how she will react toward and treat him. Then there are his feelings and her own to deal with.

In school, Jeri is often angry. She's argumentative and contrary, without meaning to be. Anger seems to catch her unexpectedly, and she's sometimes surprised by her actions. "I smart-mouth my teacher," she says. "What is the problem?" "I don't know." Pausing, she offered a justification: "I don't like when [my teacher] hurts my friends." Puffing up just a bit, she said it is important to "stand up for my friends because they are my friends." Jeri also occasionally gets into fights on the playground, and considers herself "tough," a reputation she both likes and dislikes. Speaking with a bit of bravado: "Like all my friends come to me and say, 'beat this guy up.' Sometimes I say 'no,' because I am busy doing other stuff. . . . I hate [this] . . . I really don't beat them up, but I say stuff. If they swear at me, I will swear back. . . . If they hit me, I'll hit them back."

Hoping to mitigate her anger, her teacher chose Jeri to serve as a conflict manager, a student who is trained and given a special assignment to work with other children to resolve conflicts. On the surface, the choice seemed a bit surprising, but it made good sense. By helping solve other children's playground problems, her teacher's hope was that Jeri would make progress resolving her own, and apparently she did, somewhat. Importantly, she found a good friend in her conflict manager partner, Arcelia.

Jeri isn't the only angry, disappointed child I interviewed. There were others. Katherine, a sixth-grader, is an outstanding student who enjoys reading the dictionary before going to bed, group projects, dance, and even spelling. At home, Katherine is responsible for tending her younger brother before and after school in their small apartment while her mother works full time, making certain that he doesn't answer the door unless the mother calls to tell them she is expecting a package or a visitor. Katherine takes good care of her brother. She's responsible, and her mother takes great pride in her and in her accomplishments.

Weekends are spent with Father. A normally upbeat, happy child, whose appearance reflects her disposition—colorful body glitter sprinkled around her eyes, bold earrings, and bright-blue-painted finger nails—Katherine clouded over when speaking of her father, who remarried and has a new family. She makes no bones about it; she is resentful. He's "rude," she says; and it bothers her that she has to tend his two small children, her stepbrother and stepsister. Not feeling part of her father's new family, Katherine claims she doesn't like her father, and claims she would rather avoid seeing him altogether: "I don't think my dad is very nice." Her view is that her father let her down, abandoned her and her brother in favor of two other smaller children. There is nothing she can do to change the situation, and it hurts. But as she spoke, her words echoed hollow. She misses him—badly.

In class Zeke can't sit still: antsy energy, with no direction; unbridled anger that flashes across his cherubic face.[6] When upset, and I often saw him upset, he throws horrendous, loud, huge-teared, foot-stomping, book-tossing temper tantrums; in his third-grade class he whined and complained constantly, and made great demonstrations of grief and suffering when nearly hurt or nearly slighted. His is a hostile world. When he sensed enemies closing in around him, he'd run away to a secret clubhouse he and his only friend, a classmate, built in a vacant lot where he'd hide, fume, and finally settle into an uncertain calm. I know the clubhouse, and have seen Zeke there. Other children knew to stay clear of Zeke, who was pleased to report that other kids were afraid of him; a few called him "Big Bad Zeke." He repeated the words, a warning, slowly, distinctly: "Big. Bad. Zeke." Zeke was difficult to interview: he was constantly moving, had trouble focusing, and was easily distracted. But when he did focus, he used a large vocabulary with precision. Still, I wondered at times as we spoke where he was because he most assuredly wasn't in the school library with me.

I asked Zeke about his tantrums. They're puzzling, even to him. Seeming to come from nowhere, they overwhelm him, possess him, control him, to his amazement and sometimes grief. "I don't know why," he said, straining for an explanation, and shaking his head. "I never used to be like that." Pausing, he spoke of his mother's boyfriend, whom he described as "mean." There was a connection, but it took some time to find its edge. Zeke's parents divorced not long after his birth, and a younger sister lives with the father in another state. Apparently, the boyfriend instituted rules, which Zeke didn't like at all. He concluded the boyfriend didn't like him. Besides, the man intruded into Zeke's world, standing between him and his mother, and he resented it deeply, completely. It made him angry. In class Zeke constantly spoke to his teachers of moving away from the area—so often that I was told they were surprised when he actually left Lafayette a few days after our interview for somewhere in Arizona or maybe New York; he never seemed certain where he was going, only that he would be gone, and even then he didn't always leave for more than a few days. His mother has difficulty getting and keeping jobs, and he has moved several times in his short life; but despite the difficulty, she managed to keep him at Lafayette. He doesn't make friends easily, and depends on his mother and his teachers for what little stability he can get. Yet as he spoke, it became clear that Zeke thought of himself as merely passing through Lafayette, more a visitor than an occupant.

In school and on the playground Zeke was constantly on edge, exploding and punitive when asked by his teacher to do anything outside of his wishes. Zeke rages, then collapses in tears. He speaks of death, of throwing himself off a roof to die in front of other children. In his new school, wherever that is, he probably rages still.

QUIET HURT

As noted previously, the emotions the children expressed about the men in their lives were complicated, never pure, always mixed, sometimes contradictory. Zeke's were perhaps the purest expressions: primal, desperate, wild. But even his were mixed: resentment inextricably linked with longing; a need to be loved and accepted demonstrated in destruction. Some children were less angry than quietly hurt, seemingly puzzled by events that took them away from their fathers or their fathers away from them. Two patterns emerged: acting out and withdrawal, both which deeply concern teachers. Those who withdrew longed for missing fathers and fantasized relationships they never have had. The tendency was to "freeze-frame" their fathers in time.[7] One such child is Jasmine, a shy angel-faced first-grader who seems more like an exquisitely crafted creamy chocolate-brown porcelain doll than a child. Jasmine spoke her mind.

Beautifully dressed and made up by Ronnie, her mother's young sister, a would-be manicurist, with "fake" flashy-colored jewels glued to her tiny and perfectly painted fingernails, Jasmine had difficulty describing her family for me. Men come and go; that much is clear. None apparently stay for long. Speaking in a sweet whisper, she explained that her mother was away visiting someone, she said, but she didn't approve of him, and didn't know how long she would be gone: "His name is Mike, but I don't like him very much." The family is kept together by her "Nana," a beloved grandmother who supports in the home a son dying of cancer and deteriorating rapidly; Jasmine's mother, who had difficulty keeping jobs and even more difficulty in relationships with men; Ronnie, who left school at an early age because, as Jasmine remarked, "she didn't like it very much," and who was primarily responsible for Jasmine's care.

Life is very stressful for Nana, yet she copes. Ronnie adores Jasmine, her little dress-up doll; Jasmine adores Ronnie, who is like a "sister," an older playmate rather than a mother to her.

Like Jeri, Jasmine didn't like her mother dating. "I don't like her boyfriends." "Have there been boyfriends that you liked?" "Yeah, Rob, the one that left my mom is the only one that I like. . . . He was nice and he was polite. . . . He would play with me and stuff." "He is white," she said, "but I have a black dad, but he was mean to my mom. My real dad was being mean." "Oh, what happened?" "I don't know because I was in her tummy." "Rob," she said, was her "stepdad," since he lived with her mother for what Jasmine described as a long time, perhaps more than a year, which to a 7-year-old is a very long time indeed, maybe forever. She misses Rob, wishes he were her father, but would prefer her biological father to anyone else. Jasmine accepts her mother's departure to be with Mike with some uneasiness. I wondered why. Perhaps she fears she will bring Mike home to Nana's to stay.

I asked Jasmine what she would wish for if I was an all-powerful genie and could grant her one wish, one that would make her most happy. She hesitated responding, so I posed a more direct question: "What would make you happy, Jasmine?" No smile, no doubts: "To get my dad back," she said. She hasn't seen her biological father for a "long time," but she can "still see him in her mind." "[My daddy's] nice and he plays games with me. [And he is] strong." Not angry, not bitter; Jasmine just wants her daddy. Rob might do. But not her mother's current male friend, Mike. Jasmine knows when someone does or does not care for her; and this man doesn't seem to care but her real daddy would, she believes. But her real daddy was abusive and has never been part of her life. Jasmine misses the idea of a father more than the real man.

HERE TODAY, GONE TOMORROW

Men pass quickly through Socorro's mother's life, and Socorro, a second-grade student in Mr. Lange's room, can't imagine life any differently. No anger. No disappointment. No expectations. Unstable adult relationships are normal for Socorro, although at times the rapid changes get confusing, but confusion is also normal. Socorro has multiple "daddies." Her "real" daddy, she says, lives in New York, maybe Texas soon, but he has another girlfriend, and "is not in love with my mom." She spoke softly, matter-of-factly, as though describing a commonplace site or event, a blue sky, white snow, green leaves. Nothing special. People fall in and out of love regularly, no big deal to Socorro or to her mother.

"My mommy's got two boyfriends, one is named Richardo, the other Nick." It seems that two boyfriends make life interesting. One of the two is the father of the baby her mother is carrying "in her stomach" but Socorro isn't certain which one and appears to have only modest interest in knowing although she hopes Nick, who she describes as another daddy, isn't the father: "I don't like Nick," she says, dark eyes closing slightly. Both she and her stepbrother are delighted a new baby will soon join the family. They like babies. She then mentions her "fake daddy," a fourth man, Stephen. As she talks, the relationships become increasingly complex until I found it impossible to tell which of the four men she had in mind as she spoke, except when speaking of Nick. Clearly, Nick worries her.

When interviewing Socorro's mother, Nick passed through the apartment apparently returning to work after taking a brief break. The phone rang. Socorro's 5-year-old stepbrother curled up in his mother's lap and began talking into her ear. The television was on. There is a television in every room; one is Socorro's. Cable. The apartment is spotlessly clean. Life is busy, very busy. Once off the phone, the mother exclaims, proudly, "I let her do whatever she wants . . . she does whatever she wants." Working two jobs, one in housekeeping at a nearby hospital and another, an evening job as a parking lot attendant to obtain money for a promised trip to Disneyland, leaves her no option: She is not home often. Socorro's father pays regular child support. While not at work, her mother's brother, who lives with the family and spends much of his day watching television, tends the children when they are home. Irritated, Socorro said that her uncle expects to be waited on, and she doesn't like it. "I want to support my kids," the mother says, and this requires that she is "never home for them." She works very hard.

Socorro's problem in school, her mother asserts, is that "her mind wanders." Her teachers tell another tale: Socorro cannot read and is struggling. Her mother seems unconcerned that Socorro frequently misses school. As her teacher said: "She is out of school more than she is in it." Attending school irregularly, Socorro is slipping further and further behind her classmates. Concerned, teachers made arrangements to place Socorro for part of the day with the special education teacher. They didn't know what else to do, having failed to gain the mother's help in getting Socorro to school regularly. In the special education classes the learning climate is more structured and much less complex than the regular classroom, where Socorro is so easily drawn off-task. Undisciplined, in the regular classroom Socorro ignores rules and is often in conflict with other children: "[She] has a tendency to strike first and ask questions later," her teacher quipped. In my classroom observations she seemed simply to go her own way, doing as she pleased.

Seeing or having experienced an alternative to living only with a mother, Katherine and Jeri are angered by their situation. They want something different. They know there are options. Zeke is angry at everything and everyone. His anger is indiscriminate, hot, burning anyone nearby and consuming Zeke. Socorro knows only relational chaos, which must seem normal to her, expected, the way things are supposed to be. In a sense, chaos is exciting and brings with it a kind of freedom for Socorro. But it is a phantom freedom, one that enables no refinement of expression or feeling; it is reactive, impulsive, fleeting, one grounded in a myth of living without boundaries, responsibilities, or consequences. But consequences are not recognized as connected to choices, so what an outsider might judge a consequence is no consequence at all but rather another disconnected event that happens, just like pregnancies and lover spats. Socorro is not alone. Other of the children interviewed held similar views, views that suggest they lack a sense of a tomorrow connected to today, of future.

GLAD HE'S GONE

A few of the children I spoke with were relieved their fathers were gone. Life without father is best, for his presence involved violence, drugs, and neglect. Of drugs, more will be said later. Tanner, a fragile-looking, pale fourth-grader with a serious, lined, almost gaunt old man's face, summed up the feelings of a few of the children interviewed when he said of his father, "I'm glad he is gone." He spoke without passion but with conviction. Too small to protect his mother, Tanner felt helpless as one day he watched his father try to "push [mom] off of the porch." "He was mean to my mom," Tanner said, then changed the subject. What he didn't say, but his mother said, was that he was also mean toward Tanner: "It got to the point where he was starting to get physical with Tanner; he couldn't do that with the older boys because they would have beaten the crud out of him. . . . He'd pick Tanner up and throw him across the room."

Tanner didn't want to talk of his father; he is now out of Tanner's life. Perhaps as additional time passes his father's image will move out of memory altogether, and become a shadow without substance or form, without reality, merely a faint trace of a bad dream from long ago. Tanner's mother says she hopes for nothing less.

Tanner's father struggles with serious depression. Unable to regulate his behavior, he became increasingly erratic: "When he is medicated he is okay. When he is not medicated, which is most of the time, you don't even want to be around him. He has things revealed to him, and he tells everyone off at every store he goes into. They have restraining orders against him. It is just awful. Vulgar language. . . . [Many times] the neighbors called the police. . . . " He couldn't keep jobs for more than a few days. He provided little financial support for the family, and believing that others were the origins of his difficulties, grew increasingly bitter as he found it progressively harder to get any work whatsoever. "[Tanner and his brothers] don't ever remember happiness with their dad, not ever. . . . Tanner sees that we have happiness now. [He] doesn't have to go to bed every night and put the pillow over his head and listen to screaming and yelling and fighting. We have a family . . . [and] it is good; it has been like heaven since [his father] has been gone." Observing his father's growing madness, Tanner withdrew into himself and did his best to keep out of harm's way; Tanner was left waiting, always busy but guardedly waiting, for the next explosion.

Divorce followed as the situation worsened and as the father became increasingly dangerous, but divorce did not end the difficulty. The father was out of the home but not out of the family's life. A restraining order was finally issued. With him gone the family is settled, more peaceful, and life is better for the mild-mannered Tanner who, even during the worst times before and after the divorce, never failed to do and turn in his homework and receive good marks at school. School provided a respite. His mother described him as a child who has a "lot of love in him," and who "rolls with the punches" without making any demands or holding any expectations of others. He's a survivor. School was one part of Tanner's life he could control, and he kept control there and was happy except for the one day months after the divorce when his father violated the school sanctuary, visited the playground and to Tanner's dismay had to be forcefully removed from the school grounds. The father had rented a room in a large boarding house near the school. That day, Tanner was grateful for his teachers' support and protection and mutely angry at his father who shamed him.

Tanner's mother is in no hurry to remarry, she said. Yet she thinks the "whole family would feel better if we had a functioning father in the home." "My mom died when I was five," she reveals, "so I was raised by a father, and he did a great job being a father and a mother, but there's still things that you can't do, and I can't be a father." She's grateful for a male family friend who spends time with her three sons, taking them to car shows and other places, and teaching them how to do repairs around the house. He's had, she says, a "wonderful influence on those boys," including Tanner who loves to work with him: "Tanner loves it. He just thrives on it." For now, the aim is to strengthen the family and heal. But scars are deep. Hidden. Lately the teachers have noted some uncharacteristic behavior: spitting on other children from a second-story landing as they walked below him, spewing foul words at other children, and indifference to teachers' warnings. Tanner's mother denies he's acting this way, believing other children must be the problem. His teachers know otherwise. Tanner is in trouble.

A FEW GOOD MEN

Little Dan lives with Dan, his father; Big Dan, his grandfather; and his grandmother in his grandparents' home. A first-grader, Little Dan told me he couldn't recall his mother; all he knows is what he has been told by Dan and his grandparents: "She took drugs and passed away," he says quietly but not sadly, as though her death happened in some other family. She died a few months after Little Dan's birth, just as Little Dan was beginning to take a few steps. In contrast to his grandson, Big Dan, a cheerful ruddy-faced retired railroad man with a strong and eager handshake, has clear and troubling memories of his son's girlfriend: "I hadn't seen the girl in a long time and she came to the house. She was in such a bad way that I went over to the liquor store and bought her a pint of vodka, that's what she drank most of the time. She had half of it gone in less than twenty minutes." Despite repeated warnings and occasional medical attention, Little Dan's mother drank herself to death, leaving him behind along with three daughters from two different husbands. The second husband, Big Dan said, "ran off with his daughter when she was little" in order to protect her. The two other daughters spent most of their lives in foster care, "shoved aside," Big Dan said, by their mother. Little Dan knows nothing about his sisters, only that he has them. It makes Big Dan uncomfortable to admit it, but the mother's death was a good thing, or else, he believes, Little Dan would have had a miserable life.

Little Dan, Big Dan volunteers, lowering his voice and glancing to see if the door separating us from the library is shut tightly, is "an alcohol fetal syndrome child." When Little Dan was in kindergarten the teacher told Big Dan that he had difficulty paying attention, and she wondered if he would be willing to have his eyes checked. He was. After a brief examination, the optometrist phoned Little Dan's pediatrician: "I guess you know that Little Dan is a fetal alcoholic." "Yeah," the pediatrician responded, "we know." Dan never told Big Dan; that was the first time he realized Little Dan had unique problems, and that he needed special help.[8] When Little Dan was born, he "weighed just over three pounds," Big Dan said, showing how he fit in his hand. Still small, wiry, having difficulty paying attention, and now wearing thick glasses that slip down his nose, Little Dan shows signs of fetal alcohol syndrome, but they are comparatively minor. Ritalin helps concentration, Big Dan reports, and Little Dan is making progress, which is thrilling. "I just think he is getting better all the time." Big Dan is especially grateful to Little Dan's teachers, who impress him with their skill and the care they give his grandson and the other children. A man who expresses his emotions openly, he's deeply grateful.

Two years ago, Big Dan says, he and his son came to an understanding: He and Little Dan would move into Big Dan's house. Big Dan and his wife would help care for Little Dan. Big Dan and Little Dan, in Big Dan's words, "have quite a relationship. We've walked from here to California and back, that much mileage, pushing strollers. We wore out two strollers. We walk about three or four miles a day." Each day Big Dan walks Little Dan to school; and at the day's end, Big Dan is always waiting at the classroom door to walk his grandson home. Big Dan chats with other parents waiting for their children. Everyone knows him. Seeing Big Dan and Little Dan together is wonderful, warming. As they stroll they talk about the day, and make plans for the evening. They are constantly together, and have been from the beginning. Every day for 6 weeks Big Dan visited Little Dan in the hospital. When Little Dan was born, he was in intensive care in an incubator. "I was in the nursery every day, and fed and burped him," Big Dan said. "Like I said, we had our bonding right to begin with." Later, Big Dan said, "when Little Dan was in kindergarten, there wasn't anyplace [they went] that I wasn't there with him. I would help out with the other children, too. If it was the zoo, I'd be there, or the park." Big Dan plans on always being there for Little Dan. Arriving home from school, Little Dan's grandmother helps him with his homework and reads to him. Big Dan's eyes glow bright with love as he speaks of Little Dan: "We just love him, and want to take care of him." Little Dan is Big Dan's life: Little Dan "needs help, and he is going to get it," he promises. I believe him.

Talking through lips smeared with melted dark chocolate, and revealing a new gap in his teeth, Little Dan is pleased to report on the visit of the Tooth Fairy the night before—2 dollars, not the 5 he'd hoped for. Little Dan is a happy child, quick to smile. He's excited about reading, especially *Clifford the Fire Dog*, and loves being in school. Life is good, and his grandpa and grandma make it so, especially his grandpa, whom he adores. Happily, of the caretakers of the children interviewed, Big Dan wasn't the only engaged and helpful grandpa; there were several others, grandpas and grandmas who invested significantly in the lives of their grandchildren, some of whom will be introduced later. Grandparents play a pivotal and positive role in the lives of perhaps most of the children interviewed, but most especially those doing well in school, including Katherine, Jasmine, Tanner, and Jeri, the latter who, while very young, thought her grandfather was her daddy. Nationally, more and more children are being raised by their grandparents.[9]

Big Dan wasn't the only good man in the children's lives. Roger, Jessie's stepfather, is another. Jessie, a sixth-grade student who likes to check often with her teacher just to make certain she is following directions, has a new 4-month-old baby brother. Her life has changed, and she is thrilled, in her quiet way, to talk about it. This is the family she always wanted, she said. The baby's birth quickly came to mind as the one event in her life that made her happy. "I always wanted a brother or sister," she says, and she enjoys caring for him, except when he has a "poopy diaper . . . I like it when he goes pee because it's not all gross." She'll forgive him for this little failure.

Like so many of the children interviewed, Jessie never knew her father. For the first 9 years of her life, her mother stated, "She and I did everything [together]. I was Miss Independence. I don't have any family. Most of the places I lived I didn't have any family, and it was just me and Jessie. But suddenly, this guy came into our life and we were, like, who are you to mess up our lives?" Jessie's mother fell in love. She had dated other men, even lived with one of them, but Roger is different. Because of Roger she rethought her and Jessie's futures.

Until Roger came into Jessie's life, her mother thinks she had a rather unfortunate view of marriage and of men. "My mom has been divorced for sixteen years from my stepfather, and she does not plan on getting remarried. She had a real bad experience with my stepdad. So, Jessie really hasn't seen any kind of stable marriage, until just recently. For Roger and for me it is new. For the first year of our marriage we were struggling through all sorts of changes, but since [our son] has been born things have settled down. Things are getting better. We moved into a new house. I've always worried about what her picture of marriage is, what her picture of a married couple is, and hopefully we can give her a good one." She spoke enthusiastically about the future.

Jessie's stepfather, her mother said, is filled with love. A photographer, his pictures of children move her deeply, and she is proud of what he does: "He sees kids for who they are. He can see their love in their hearts and their happiness and joy, and that is what he catches on film. [He is] wonderful with children," she says lovingly. He is patient with Jessie, corrects her gently, even after she rudely answers his business line and offends a client, and is mindful of the complex feelings she is still working through with the marriage and the baby's birth. He takes her to school each morning across town, and they talk and laugh as he drives. The drive is necessary since the move from the neighborhood into the new house. Jessie attends Lafayette to minimize the impact of so many changes taking place at once in her life; life is complex but good and getting better.

For Jessie's mother, the changes of the past several months have been dramatic: "I am a clothing designer," she said. "I did some traveling. . . . I would have to fly from Boston to New York and back in the same day and try to get it inside the day care hours. I would come home exhausted, having driven through Boston traffic. It would take me an hour and a half [to settle down]. I was yelling at the traffic by the time I was close to home [from the airport], and day care was always mad at me. Jessie kind of got shuffled around between people that I could find to take care of her. Eventually I had to leave the job because I just couldn't do that to her. She was too little, and we didn't have any family to help." She commented on the effects on children of being shuffled around: "I feel bad for these kids, in some ways it really hurts them." She forged another career in business, but quit prior to the birth of the baby, deciding with Roger that she wanted to enjoy her son and be a "stay-at-home mom for a while." Jessie is happy, still "bossy," her mother says, but happy, more happy than she has ever been. Her mother is also happy. Life is very good.

REFLECTIONS

Half of all children will live in a single-parent home before the age of 18. About two thirds of African-American children are born out of wedlock. Nearly 6 in 10 children under 6 years old, who live with a single mother, are in poverty. Very young mothers often lack basic skills needed to find desirable work, and welfare is not a long-term solution. Finding their income drop on average by over one fifth immediately following divorce, formerly married mothers who have not been in the workforce must find employment, and the work they find not only takes them away from their children, but also too seldom fills the income gap created by the father's departure. Even when child-support payments are regular, they are often small. Little wonder so many children are under severe stress.[10]

Divorce may resolve some problems, but others follow. As mentioned, children of divorce wonder if they had a part in their parents' splitting up. Feelings of rejection often tarry, and sometimes express themselves in anger and acting out in the classroom and on the playground. Emotional problems frequently persist into adulthood. Many of the children interviewed never knew their fathers, and these children have additional challenges. They fantasize about a father, create images of what their dad would have been like, most assuredly, if he were in the home. But he is not. Often the children have no idea where their fathers are, and the sense of absence is profound and ever-present.

School performance improves when two adults are available to remind a child to do her or his homework or to assist with a report. Many mothers succeed in creating a stable loving home with clear expectations, like Katherine's and Jeri's mothers, but work pressures and complex family relationships often interfere with their best efforts, and to some degree children suffer. They suffer not only because they frequently do not get help at home, but because of the burdens they must carry—burdens that for some children interfere with concentrating at school, completing and turning in assignments, and sometimes even attending regularly. Uncertainty is internalized, stability desperately needed by some. Socorro's mind was as disorganized as her mother's home life. So was Zeke's. When his teacher, Mrs. Novakovich, glued herself to Zeke he accomplished something in class—not much, but something. Twenty-four other children needed her assistance, however, so she could rarely attend to Zeke as he needed. But then Zeke couldn't and wouldn't tolerate such closeness even if it could have been offered consistently. Zeke needed space. He didn't know how to care for other people or to accept offers of kindness. No trust. No confidence. To some degree, grandpas and grandmas can fill in, and when they do they can make a hugely positive difference in the lives of children; generally these children of those interviewed performed better in school, but only when the grandparents contributed to stability, and not all did.

For two decades it has been common to argue that children do fine without fathers. We now know otherwise.[11] Children desperately need daddies who help them confidently confront the world, whose principles when internalized become the content of conscience, of superego. Psychologically, boys need loving but firm fathers to help them separate from their mothers, channel aggression, and gain tempered strength so that later they may reconnect, not as needy children searching for a mother, but as men who accept responsibility to care for and protect those they love and who confidently enjoy the company of women. Girls need their daddies, too, and daddies' forms of caring and nurturing that build competence, courage, and a sense of trust and security, a sense that the world outside of the home is a decent place, a place where human agency matters. The evidence is compelling: Young women with divorced or separated parents are more likely than others to leave home at a young age, form a union, have a child, and have a child out-of-wedlock.

Male and female patterns of play differ with children. The patterns are complementary. Mothers tend to reach down to a child and play at their level, while fathers tend to emphasize individualism and competition. Fathers expect children to play their games, games fathers enjoy, and in the process both girls and boys build confidence and empathy, and learn about limitations. In addition, the evidence is quite persuasive that men encourage a sense of competence in children because of their strong concern for what their children do, their achievement. Often the child-father relationship takes the form of a kind of apprenticeship: the father teaches the child how to do something. In contrast, mothers tend to be most concerned with how children feel, with their emotional well-being. Jeri, Katherine, and Jasmine desperately wanted fathers; Jessie got one, and according to her mother for the first time in her life began to see new possibilities for love and growth within the tension of male-female relationships.[12]

This said, there is no doubt that some children are better off without their biological fathers, men who made babies but failed as fathers. But these children still need men in their lives, able, loving, and morally centered men.[13] Jeri's mom knows this, as she searches for a husband to be a father to Jeri.

One of the best predictors, perhaps the best, of a child's success in school is parental involvement in the child's learning. In fact, when parents are involved students achieve more regardless of their ethnic, racial, or socioeconomic background. And two involved parents are better than one, whether or not the parents are married. Wishes to the contrary, teachers cannot make up for disengaged parents, or for missing fathers; they and the children suffer the consequences: classroom expressions of anger, hurt, rejection, betrayal, fear, confusion, worthlessness, and guilt. But teachers can help by easing the way of parents into the school and classroom, and when they do and do so as a matter of school policy and faculty commitment, children, especially those who are most behind, benefit immensely. Lafayette teachers made Herculean efforts to involve the children's guardians in their child's education, from daily planners, to sponsoring a yearly community Halloween night, to home visits. The teachers also did their part by making certain school was safe, secure, and the curriculum positive and appropriately challenging, a place where children can and will learn if they attend regularly and if they work. Engaged parents of other children also help, as do children who seldom misbehave and who facilitate teachers' learning goals and help create positive school and classroom cultures. Some of these children are from single-parent homes and doing well in school, children like Katherine. But there are fewer and fewer such parents and children at Lafayette, indeed in all urban schools. Many financially able neighborhood parents have abandoned the public schools by placing their offspring in private schools where there are few struggling children and some have placed their children in other schools with more stable student populations or in the district-sponsored gifted-and-talented program composed mostly of white middle- and upper-middle-class children from supportive two-parent homes. One of these programs is housed inside Lafayette. Student numbers have not diminished, but the numbers of children who are "needy," as the teachers say, and whose problems are increasingly severe, have increased.

Mommies, Daddies, and Drugs

As I write, I have in front of me a *Washington Post* story written by Peter Selvin and William Claiborne dated March 1, 2000: "1st Grader Shoots Classmate to Death." Kayla Rolland was shot and killed at the Theo J. Buell Elementary School in Flint, Michigan, by her classmate who apparently was upset with her following a playground disagreement. The boy, whose father is in prison for drug charges and who lived with his mother in a crack house, got the loaded and stolen weapon from an uncle at the house. Selven and Claiborne write: "Family service workers were trying to learn whether the boy and a younger sibling had been neglected, and whether they should be removed from their home." A remarkable statement.

It is well-known that drugs, alcohol, and crime go together. Eighty percent of the men incarcerated in the state penitentiary are there for having committed alcohol- or drug-related crimes. Drinking is involved in about 40 percent of the rapes and sexual assaults in the nation. Thirty-eight percent of those convicted of murder had been drinking at the time they committed their crime. Prisoners are also parents. About 200,000 American children have an imprisoned mother and more than 1.6 million have an imprisoned father.[1] What is less well-known is that there is a direct and powerful relationship between child neglect and abuse and drug and alcohol usage. At least half of all substantiated cases of child abuse involve caregiver alcohol or drug abuse.[2]

In the days following the shooting of Kayla Rolland, the father of the boy who shot her was interviewed in prison. He expressed his regret for not being more involved in the boy's life but said there wasn't much he could do. Kayla's teacher cried. In this chapter, three of the four fathers discussed are in prison, including Alfredo's.

THE CHILDREN

Alfredo

I'd heard about Alfredo before I met him. Younger children in the neighborhood think he is a gangster; older boys disdainfully refer to him as a "wanna-be," a kid who looks like a gangster, but isn't. Short, square-headed, and dressed usually in dark baggy clothes, Alfredo has "attitude," and older children in the neighborhood comment on his foul mouth and quick temper. He seems to be a boy looking for a beating. Like Juan from Mrs. Sorensen's class, he swaggers, he's argumentative, and his mouth runs ahead of his mind when he is stirred up. But he is also very, very bright. "Oh, he is brilliant, a smart kid," his teacher remarked, and he is.

Looking at Alfredo without knowing him, he's easily dismissed as just another street kid looking for trouble. But Alfredo surprises. He has a large vocabulary, keeps up on world events by making certain he watches the late evening news each day, and worries about his and his family's safety. "When I lived in Los Angeles, I always thought someone was going to come up and shoot me," he says, and he still worries: he's wary, always on guard. "It makes me [nervous], that someone is going to come up and grab me. . . . I have seen this guy [near our apartment] two times. He is really suspicious; he comes around a lot and [watches] me and my little brother play football." Alfredo is especially concerned about his younger mentally handicapped brother's safety. Christian easily gets into trouble, and Alfredo's responsibility is to get him out. Since an older brother was incarcerated in a juvenile detention facility, Christian has been Alfredo's responsibility, particularly while his mother is away working late hours as a maid. Wherever Alfredo goes, so goes Christian, a tagalong, glued to his coattail.

Alfredo tells those who ask that his father is a long-haul truck driver who is away from home a lot. When we chatted the older brother was in "lock-up because he did a crime." It upsets Alfredo that his father and brother are in prison, and so he avoids the subject: "It's too hard [to talk about]." He's not embarrassed by them, however. He admires them both. It may have been hard to talk with me because of who I am, an adult whom he assumes makes quick and unfavorable judgments about prisoners, and he probably is right—as I said, Alfredo is bright. With his mother working long hours, Alfredo is raising himself and his brother. A sister and her boyfriend also live in the small two-room apartment, but they have little involvement in his life. At age 12 Alfredo is on his own.

Alfredo likes Lafayette a lot. "I've changed my attitude; now I get better grades. I am not a fool anymore. [Where I came from] there was nothing but fools, like I was. [No one] taught [me] anything. . . . I just failed because I didn't want to keep learning the same thing, the same thing, same thing, same thing." What Alfredo didn't know is that the teachers at Lafayette met periodically to discuss his progress, and made adjustments to help him have better, more positive relationships with the students and adults in the school, including making provision for him to work each day in the library as an aide, which gave him responsibility, a bit of power, and a relationship with a thoughtful, caring adult. He loved his time in the library. They also sought to keep him separated from his friend Randall who was introduced previously. When these two friends were together trouble followed, especially on the playground. What Alfredo understood was that at Lafayette he was treated differently, and that the context was different: "There is no trouble here. [Where I was before this year] there was stealing, there was shootings, there was all this kind of stuff, you know. I was always around it. I had to be a bad person [there]. . . . I like this school because it is a better environment for me. . . . [I've] learned a lot more than I did." He was thrilled that he had 15 pages of his research report completed, "the most in the whole class," and was very pleased with himself: "I am proud of myself. I like it." Remarkably, Alfredo was especially appreciative that his teacher plans for the school day, apparently a new experience: "Before he wakes up in the morning, he'll say, 'I'm going to go to school and I am going to have my kids do this in the morning, then we are going to go to the assembly. We are going to do this, that, and we are going to have a good day.'" I didn't ask Alfredo about teacher planning; only about what he liked about the school. He thought of planning.

Alfredo is aware of his reputation, which troubles him. Shortly after Christmas for the first time in the school's history some student backpacks were stolen from the hallway where they were hanging. Teachers were amazed and distressed. Children were upset. Mrs. Sorensen gave impassioned lectures on honesty, on how "we don't do that" here. Such things simply do not occur in Lafayette; they're unthinkable. Knowing he and his little brother were relatively new to the school, he feared others would blame him, and a few of his classmates apparently did: "Yeah, that is what they were saying. Me [and Randall] and my little brother are pretty much the only kids that came new from the school so I don't want nobody blaming me. But I doubt they are because my backpack got stolen, so why would I want to be stealing backpacks?" Still, he was concerned; he didn't want an accusatory finger pointing his way even for a second. Alfredo has a lively sense of justice.

After interviewing Alfredo, his older brother was released from detention. A "low point" followed, his teacher said. "[The brother] loaded Alfredo with a bunch of gang talk, and [talk about how] everything is unfair, [how he is discriminated against]. Alfredo was really angry for a few weeks. But the brother . . . got arrested [again] because there were some outstanding warrants. . . . Alfredo was really upset. . . . I finally found [the theme song for the television show] *Baretta*. 'Don't do the crime if you can't do the time.' I played that. He understood. . . . [We

talked, and he calmed down]." Alfredo's relationship with Randall continues to trouble his teacher: "When there are people around Alfredo who
know how to push his buttons, and make him mad, he [gets] out of
control."

While pondering Alfredo's future, Mr. DeCourse slowly shook his
head from side to side, discouraged by what he envisioned: "I think he
is wonderful, but he is [likely to be] a monster kid. What chance is he
going to have?" He especially worries that junior high school will fail
miserably with this bright child, who "doesn't have any family support."
"He needs [to have fewer teachers], and people who understand where
he is, where he is going. [But junior high school teachers] are going to
have one hundred twenty kids at least. They are not even going to look.
He is going to end up like the gangsters over there [at that school] and
end up getting kicked out. I worry about that, but what can I do? I have
tried to give him as many tools as I can, note taking, how to write reports,
how to study. But I haven't been able to touch [what he really needs],
how to stay calm, cool, collected. I haven't been able to do that. . . . [With
his two friends he still] gets into a fight mode at the drop of a hat." The
danger is that Alfredo will be written off before being given a chance, a
gang-wanna-be who cares for his handicapped brother and who dreams
that one day he will be able to help the "handicapped, disabled so they
can work and live with their families and not care homes. . . . My best
friend," he said, "his mom, her brother, half of his brain was fried when
he was a baby so he got really weird. . . . I just figured, maybe I could
[help]."

Alfredo has grown up with adults who abuse alcohol and use illegal
drugs. Drugs appear to be part of life. Mixing alcohol or illegal drugs
with buttons that are easily pushed and a quick temper eventually may
well produce the "monster" child Mr. DeCourse fears Alfredo will become, a child like Alfredo's father and his older brother apparently were.
For now, Alfredo swears he does not drink or take drugs of any sort.

Josiah

Josiah lives with his father's mother, who works long hours at a nearby
7–11 convenience store, and his stepgrandfather. Before I interviewed
Josiah, we chatted whenever I observed in class as well as often in the
hallway. I also helped with practices of the fourth-grade play he was in.
He befriended me immediately, and while sitting observing in class he'd
show me his drawings, mostly of dragons, sometimes of airplanes or
spacecraft, for my approval. Being with Josiah is exhausting. Hooks go in,
and he cannot let go; any adult who shows interest in him is immediately

a best friend for life. A bumptious boy, Josiah doesn't know how to be-friend children, and in his aggressive pursuit of friendship alienates and drives away even the most willing. In class, his teacher said, he's often "obnoxious." He burps out loud, makes strange noises, talks loudly, has difficulty keeping his hands to himself, and distracts other children, all the while seeking their approval, a smile, a nod. He'll have a good friend for a week, perhaps two, then a painful separation follows for Josiah as his now former friend seeks relief, a bit of breathing space. Josiah is suffocating, as I quickly discovered.

Anger sometimes follows rejection, rejection that comes, Josiah firmly believes, because of his "red hair and freckles." "I hate them," he says passionately. He also thinks others don't like him because of his large stature; he's likely the biggest and tallest fourth-grade student in Lafayette. "They call me 'flubber'; it means I'm fat." He isn't. Things would be better, he insists, if he was "more handsome . . . not as many freckles and red hair."[3] He seems unaware that his driving pursuit of friendship coupled with his large size sometimes frightens other children. His strength easily gets away from him, but he doesn't mean it to. Nor does he realize how often his classroom behavior irritates his classmates who ignore or occasionally grimace rather than laugh at his antics.

Josiah's parents live in a trailer park in a nearby city. His 9-year-old sister lives with his mother's mother. Desperately, Josiah wants to be with his sister, but cannot. "I dream about being with my sister," he says, longingly. Surely she would be a friend, a true friend. When he was a baby, he said his mother took his sister to his grandmother's house because the mother was "scared to be with us." I asked Josiah if he knew why; he said he had "no idea." As we continued to talk, however, he became more comfortable and open: "My dad is drinking alcohol and sometimes my mom will drink. . . . My mom and dad smoke pot most of the time. . . . My dad made me drink on New Year's Eve." Stunned, I asked, "He did what?" "My dad made me drink on New Year's Eve . . . when I was nine. . . . He made me. He was drunk. I was playing with my friends. . . . I told my dad, 'No,' but he made me. He said, 'If you don't, I'll beat the heck out of you.' . . . [In the morning] I had a headache." "But you didn't do anything wrong, Josiah." "My dad did."

Life in the trailer was chaos, Josiah says. No rules. Josiah and a friend watched television at all hours while his parents slept or partied. The family moved frequently, and Josiah has attended "four thousand schools," or "about ten." He doesn't know for certain how many. Now his life is more stable with his grandmother, but his stepgrandfather is cause for concern: He drinks heavily and his grandmother attempts to shield Josiah from his stepgrandfather's ill temper when drinking. "My grandpa, all he does is sit down and drink his vodka, and then he'll go and sit on the couch and watch T.V." The grandmother explained to his teacher that she tries to help Josiah cope with her husband's outbursts: She says to him, his "are empty words. Whenever he is rude, I say watch his mouth Josiah, they come out of his mouth and they go up in the air and they disappear. I tell him not to pay attention to them. They are not going to hurt you. They are gone as soon as they are out of his mouth." The grandmother is Josiah's greatest support: "I really love Josiah; the one thing he has going for him is that he knows that I love him." It seems the stepgrandfather would rather not be a parent. Raising grandchildren is stressful.[4]

The grandparents live in a one-bedroom apartment in an older building in the center of town. Both work. Josiah sleeps on the couch in the living room. He reports that he has a few toys, which he keeps in a bucket in the corner of the living room, and a few items are stored behind his grandmother's overstuffed chair. He keeps the room clean. Toys are not left out. After Josiah does his chores, which includes washing the dishes, and does his homework—he's a good student—he is allowed to watch television with his stepgrandfather. This is how he spends his evenings. Life is lonely. Uncertain. But better than it was—of that he has no doubts.

After our interview I walked Josiah home. He yammered, thrilled we were together and I was paying attention. When we reached the apartment building, Josiah insisted I come in to see his drawings and his toys. Gently I explained to him that I couldn't, that I wouldn't want to do anything that would cause a problem for him, or for me. His grandparents weren't home yet. He seemed to understand, and after unlocking the front door, turned, smiled broadly, and waved good-bye. Had I ventured in, he would have shown me each of his toys, one at a time, and each of his drawings, and told me about them while scouring my face for signs of interest, as he had done in class.

Arcelia

Josiah's classmate Arcelia also lives with her grandparents, her mother's mother and stepfather, a police officer. They live several miles from Lafayette, a 30-minute drive, but Arcelia is kept in the school because, as she says, "I have been to too many schools." Her grandparents have stabilized Arcelia's life. She is happy. Busy. Going to school, which she loves. Playing soccer. Doing chores. Playing with friends. Working on her computer. Listening to music. Baking cookies with and teasing her high-school-age stepaunt who is more like an older sister. As she speaks, it is difficult to imagine that this whispering, charmingly shy, small, wide-eyed girl has had such a hard life. Her innocence belies her experience.

There is a remarkable clinical quality to Arcelia's description of her parents, as though she is reading from a magazine a story about dysfunctional parents. No change in inflection; no change in expression. Just the facts: "My dad went to jail because he was doing drugs and my mom was doing drugs but she is [out of jail]." "Your dad is still in jail now, then?" I asked. "Yep . . . He was doing [drugs] and he steals." Her mother, she said, is now living with a sister. She visited her father in jail a few weeks before we spoke. She doesn't have much hope for his future: "He thinks he is off drugs, but he never really gets off. My dad, he lives with, well, whenever he kind of gets off drugs, he lives with my grandma." The parents were married, divorced, remarried, and are now getting divorced again. For Arcelia these developments do not appear particularly newsworthy.

It is important to Arcelia to do well in school. Her grandparents expect it, and so does she. She said at the beginning of the year that she didn't do her homework as faithfully as she should have, but she does now. One reason is that she was chosen to be a conflict manager, and her partner is Jeri, introduced in the previous chapter. "I started doing conflict managing and [my teacher] said—I like to do conflict managing— she scared me by saying, 'If you don't put in your homework, then the next time you don't put in your homework, then I'm not going to [allow you] to be a conflict manager anymore. I decided to do my homework and I have been doing my homework ever since." She's a good student now, and getting better. She and Jeri take being conflict managers seriously, and both enjoy the authority and responsibility that come with the position.

Arcelia loves her teacher. What she liked best about her teacher surprised me: "She does discipline." "She does discipline?" "Yeah." "What is discipline?" "It is when you don't have to be a spoiled brat and you don't get everything that you want and stuff like that. I have really, when I lived with my mom and dad I didn't really get that much discipline, although I wouldn't really get to see them, so it wouldn't really be that much difference." Puzzled, I asked: "When you were living with them you didn't get to see them?" "Well, I would get to see them but they would mostly hide in the bathroom because they were doing drugs. . . . They wouldn't wake me up [for school] because they were asleep because half of the time they were mostly having a party or something. So I really didn't get that much discipline when I was with my mom and dad. Then when I moved to my grandma and grandpa, because they found out what was happening, they always knew . . . but this time, well, my grandma, she knew that they would go back on drugs when I was born so she said to my mom and my dad that she would have me every single weekend because they were not doing anything [to take care of me]. I would have to make my own food. . . . She knew that one day she was going to take me because she wanted me to have a better life." Children of parents who abuse drugs typically assume caretaking roles for themselves and rarely receive helpful parental guidance or have reasonable and stable disciplinary boundaries.[5] Arcelia is grateful for discipline, for rules and for adults who stand behind them and enforce them, for her teacher and for her grandparents. Life is better when there are rules, and when rules are enforced. A bright but antsy second-grade student I interviewed with an attention deficit disorder echoed Arcelia's thoughts: "I just like the rules that we have. They are good rules. . . . I really want to behave."

Life is good now, but Arcelia fears the future. "If my grandma and grandpa dies. . . . They said that I shouldn't be worried because I have my Aunt Martha and relatives, [but] I was scared. I am still scared because I don't really want to go back and live with my mom until she is really, really, off drugs. I don't want to have a life like that again. I have been kind of scared. My mom said that I don't really need to be, well she said it is alright for me to be scared. . . . My mom says that [I get scared] probably because of [them]. The houses that we used to live in, like there would be a lot of people there and sometimes [my parents' roommate's daughter would] have a new father. Or [my cousins] had a really bad life because, well they still have a bad life because Jerry he got molested. Lydia, she goes to every single guy, giving herself away for drugs. . . . [She's] my dad's sister. I had another aunt . . . she doesn't really do that much drugs but she did drugs. . . . " Drugs are everywhere. Parents. Aunts and lovers. One of the lovers molested Jerry, she said: "He molested Jerry, and he would slap us and hit us for no reason. He was just really, really, mean. The reason that [my aunt] liked him is because he would give her a lot of money and she would spend that for drugs. I think that he was doing drugs." Little wonder Arcelia worries about losing her grandparents.

Being away from her parents and in her grandmother's loving home cannot completely erase Arcelia's fears. Her mother often disappoints her, and she cries, burying her face in a pillow. She tells Arcelia to call, and when she does, her mother isn't home. But most of all, Arcelia worries that one day she will get a stepdad, perhaps like the man who molested Jerry.

Shane

Shane sparkles. He's 6 years old, missing a couple of teeth, and, according to his teacher, is "Mr. Social." Because he often doesn't complete his work, he is in the bottom of the higher reading group. He's often off-task, but he is bright, engaging: His teacher said he "would rather play around, he [prefers] talking to his friends" to working on his assignments. When I interviewed him he was looking forward to when his new front teeth would begin to come in. Speaking with Shane, no one would imagine that this bright, talkative child, a child who chats happily with friends on the rug in the middle of the classroom or helps another child with his math after having completed his own assignment, was a drug baby, born 6 weeks early by way of cesarian section. Drug babies aren't supposed to be so bright, so alive. But he is.

When as a small child Shane came to live with his grandmother, who, with his stepgrandfather, is his legal guardian, he slept under their bed, and kept his toys and food there for over a year. He was afraid of something, but his grandparents are not certain exactly what. They know that he had seen his father break his mother's arm. They know that gang members hung around the house, and Shane, in diapers, was on his own while his parents slept. They know that he was afraid of losing his toys because so often he lost them as his parents moved from place to place. They know he spent a great deal of time alone, thinking; he still spends time on his own thinking and he surprises them with his self-sufficiency, his need to solve problems independently.

As we spoke, Shane's grandmother told of her life, a tale I had not expected to hear. A methamphetamine addict, she gave custody of her own infant daughter to her mother. She quit taking drugs only when she discovered she was 6 1/2 months pregnant. Later, she became a heroin addict, only quitting when meeting her current husband 10 years ago: "It came down to the drugs or him. I had to learn how to be treated good. I am still learning but I finally learned to trust again, thanks to [my husband]. He is a good and loving man that stood by me through all kinds of hell." She entered drug rehab, and with her husband's help has, she said, been "clean" for 7 years, since before Shane's birth. Several times she nearly died from overdoses. Because of Shane, both quit drinking, and the grandmother quit smoking: "Shane came to me and he said, 'Grandma, why do you drink that whiskey?' He really hit me . . . I stopped."

I asked about Shane's mother. For 6 years she was raised by her grandmother but then went to live with her father who was given legal custody. Shane's grandmother shared her reasoning for giving up her daughter: "I had this image that [the stepmother] was a lady and would give [my daughter] a family environment [and that my daughter] would know her dad like I never [knew mine]. My dad . . . was an alcoholic and beat me and my brother. . . . He went to Tokyo to run a club and to Vietnam. I didn't see him [for many years]. Anyway, [my daughter] went to live with her dad. . . . [My daughter eventually] brought them up on abuse charges. Apparently [her stepmother] had got into drugs along with her dad . . . methamphetamine. Cocaine and methamphetamine . . . It is what they call 'crank.' . . . I have been on every drug in the world . . . speed . . . tiny white meth pills with crosses on them. I actually shot those. That was my first experience with needles." She began giving me a lesson on drug usage, a complex lesson: "What that [methamphetamine usage] does to you, is you don't sleep. You don't eat. You are up a long time and your brain goes to a place of nothing, of fear and paranoia. . . . You [can] party and work. You get this feeling like you can do anything even though you really don't do anything but the wig. You'll get into a box to straighten out or a cupboard or something. You will tear it all out but you never get it organized." She continued: "You also hallucinate. You hear things and see things that aren't there. Like most cocaine addicts and meth addicts will shut their doors and windows, curtains and stuff, and they will say 'they are watching me. I know they are watching me, the police. There is somebody out there.' . . . I have done acid, all that stuff. Methamphetamine is the most dangerous drug there is to our society because there is no connection to reality. At least on heroin or pain pills, opiates, you are down so you are not out killing and robbing. . . . "

Shane's mother ran away, taking with her some of her father and stepmother's drugs. She got her first drugs from her stepmother's sister. The relationship between father and daughter struck Shane's stepgrand-father as sick: "They are more like lovers [than father and daughter] because they do drugs together." The daughter dropped out of school in seventh grade, and has been in and out of drug treatment, paid for by the stepgrandfather, ever since. At age 16 she gave birth to Shane.

Shane's father, the child of a prostitute, gained his 15 minutes of fame by going on a shooting rampage on the freeway while high on methamphetamine, wounding two men. In prison, he will be out of Shane's life for some years, which is seen by Shane's grandparents as a good outcome. They consider him intellectually dull and dangerous. On the other hand, his mother moves in and out of Shane's life, and each time leaves behind wounds. Unlike his grandparents and teachers, she makes promises, but doesn't keep them consistently. Fearing they might lose custody, Shane's grandparents allow him to spend some weekends with his mother who is currently living with a boyfriend who deals marijuana, in a town an hour away: "If he goes to [stay] . . . we'll pick him up and he is filthy. I mean, just filthy." They know that the mother, who is on probation, is dealing drugs again, and they hope she will be arrested. They are especially pleased that Shane seems to be "losing that fantasy about her, [about] living with her. He enjoys the time on the weekends [when they are together] because he gets to stay up late, eat junk food, be bums." Being with his mother is quite an adventure, according to Shane. She works at a fast food restaurant, and he gets "kid's meals" that he likes. He also gets excited about seeing his mother's three snakes, the boyfriend's cat, and his two pets, a snake and a rat. Despite the excitement, his grandparents think life with his mother "is losing its luster, because he has seen that life can be better. . . . I think it is important that he gets to know her so that he doesn't have [an] illusion [about her]." What they don't know is that Shane doesn't like her boyfriend; a fact that would please them immensely if they knew. Still, the grandparents are fearful that she might take them to court and gain custody of Shane again. If that were to happen, the grandmother promises, she will take him and run: "Someone has got to fight for this young man," she says passionately. She means it.

The grandfather spends part of each day doing homework with Shane, which pleases Shane: "I like to do my homework," he says, meaning he likes to work with his grandpa. They talk. And they go to his various activities together: summer programs at the university, gymnastics, soccer, tennis lessons, fishing, archery, karate, and skiing. He's a very busy 6-year-old. Both grandparents are especially interested in his school activities. They love Lafayette. Until suffering a major setback in his business, Shane's stepgrandfather thought seriously about placing him in a private school, but Shane insisted he didn't want to go. "Lafayette," he said, "is my school." He's doing reasonably well academically, and fabulously well socially. They appreciate Shane's teachers and the school principal, especially when they feared Shane's mother would "yank him out of school," and found themselves needing help: "They were very helpful, cooperative with that, and watching him."

Listening to Shane's grandparents, I was struck by the passion with which they spoke of him and by the intensity of their commitment. "Has there ever been a boy loved more?" I asked. "I don't think so," his grandmother responded. "I think that we both feel that he is a special kid from God. He has a special purpose. He has given us far more than we could ever give him. . . . God loans us our children. They don't belong to us." For his part, Shane asserts that his grandpa is his second daddy.

Despite the pain caused by his parents, when I asked what would make him happiest, just one wish, Shane said, "That my mom and dad

would be back together." I wasn't surprised, but his grandparents would
be heartbroken.

REFLECTIONS

Of the 34 children interviewed, half had parents or stepparents with
drug-related problems, problems that severely and negatively affected
the quality of their lives. Drug and alcohol abuse is pervasive and devastating to families and children, where there is an ineluctable link with child
maltreatment. In the District of Columbia Family Court in 1995, two of
three parents of abused and neglected children tested positive for cocaine;
one in seven tested positive for heroin and other opiates. Forty states
report that one of the top two problems of families reported for mistreating
children is parental substance abuse.[6] A recent Columbia University study
concluded that children of parents who use drugs and alcohol are three
times more likely to be neglected than other children, and four times as
likely to be abused. In Utah the Department of Human Services reports
that half of the child neglect cases are related to perinatal drug and alcohol
use. Drug and alcohol treatment is needed by more than two thirds of
parents involved with the child welfare system.[7] Those entering treatment
are younger and younger and gender differences are blurring. Women
are nearly as likely as men to have substance abuse problems.

About half a million children are being cared for outside of their
immediate families: children like Shane, Arcelia, and Josiah; but there are
not nearly enough placements to meet the growing need. It is estimated
that 60 percent of these children have moderate to severe mental health
problems, but few receive needed care. Shane did. Grandmothers and
grandfathers often step in and attempt to repair the damage caused by
their children to their grandchildren. Grandparents like Shane's are bro-
kenhearted as they speak of their children: there are lots of regrets and
hope for redemption.

These childrens' grandparents provide stability, love, and support,
and because of them each of their grandchildren is doing well in school
and the future appears promising. In them children find firm anchors
that can sustain identity and secure the self. The children recognize that
their lives are better because of their grandparents and are aware of their
parents' failings. Too young to fully understand the mess his parents
have made of their lives, only Shane longs to be back with his parents,
while both Josiah and Arcelia worry that someday they will have to
return. Grandparents also fret. Given the general unwillingness of courts
to rule against biological parents' claims on their children, they worry

that they will not be able to raise these children before they are taken away from them. Perhaps Shane will feel differently as he matures, but for now his grandparents take comfort in what they believe is his growing recognition of his mother's instability and unreliability, each a product of a life controlled by drug usage for nearly 10 years, almost half of his mother's life. Once strikingly beautiful, she looks much older than her 23 years; the skin on her face is badly scarred by methamphetamine use and she has no direction, no skills, and no possible way of supporting her son financially let alone emotionally. Shane doesn't realize any of this. He's 6 years old. These grandparents are at war with their own children, and they think they have very few allies. Perhaps they are right. But teachers are allies, people who support the cause of children, who proved themselves to Shane's grandparents.

Alfredo struggles. On the one hand he recognizes that both his father and older brother are criminals, but he loves them both and desperately wants to believe they are not wholly to blame for their circumstances; they are victims of an unfair judicial system, as they claim. I am reminded of the 1919 World Series scandal, when a young fan said to Shoeless Joe Jackson, "Say it ain't so, Joe." But it is: Alfredo doesn't want to believe what he knows is true. His teacher helped him confront a painful truth.

When I began interviewing I had not anticipated that so many children's lives would be harmed by parental illegal drug usage. I thought there would be some, but not this much, not this many fractured lives. Several families have disintegrated. Poverty follows illegal drug usage, sexual and physical abuse, and sometimes incarceration. But the impact on children is not always readily apparent; damage is beyond the reach of researchers. Data are scant and the picture of the damage far from complete. Despite his progress, because his mother drank heavily throughout her pregnancy Little Dan has physical impairments that impede his ability to learn. Similarly, Marshall, a second-grade boy who will be introduced later, was born with severe learning disabilities and permanent neurological damage that profoundly and adversely affects his ability to perform in school; he looks healthy, but he isn't. Others live in fear. Shane slept under his grandparents' bed and hoarded food; so did Brad, one of the children introduced from Mrs. Sorensen's class, whose mother was an addict. Arcelia has bad dreams, nightmares about returning to live with her parents. Counseling has helped a few of the children, but counseling is not widely available and is no substitute for living in supportive and loving environments and for time to heal, both aims of these grandparents.

Like many American schools, Lafayette has only a part-time counselor, who cannot possibly respond to all the children in need, let alone their parents. Like it or not, teachers often find themselves in counseling roles, but mostly their task is to protect the children, cooperating as they can with guardians, and to make certain their classes are caring places where children live bounded lives where decency and civility are taught and reinforced. Recall Arcelia's appreciation of discipline, of rules. Even Alfredo responded to the consistency of the culture created in Lafayette. While he was in class, inside the building, inside the library, he behaved in ways consistent with the culture and supportive of his own learning. He performed. He was pleased with himself. He was building competence. What worried his teacher, Mr. DeCourse, was what would happen to Alfredo once he left the school.

Few of the drug dependent adults in these children's lives success-fully completed drug rehabilitation programs, of which there are far too few, costs are far too high, and delays for entry far too long—often more than 10 months, 10 months when children are bounced around an overburdened child care system.[8] Results of such programs are often depressing, but there are promising developments, particularly for women. Comprehensive treatment programs are cost-effective, resulting in uncomplicated drug-free births, reduced dependency on welfare, and dramatic decreases in criminal activity. In addition, when children partici-pate with their mothers in treatment, school performance improves. Such programs include child care, which traditional programs, often designed for men, ignore. Keeping one's children motivates many women to com-plete such programs and remain drug-free.[9] Men absent from their families have no such motivation. This said, prevention is the key.

CHAPTER 5

Abuse in the Home

Abuse takes many forms, including sexual and physical, as well as domestic violence and emotional maltreatment.[1] Physical neglect is the most common form of child maltreatment, accounting for about 60 percent of all reported cases. Neglect is what Arcelia experienced. But categories within abuse are not discrete, nor is the border separating abuse from neglect clearly marked. What is clear is that many children experience multiple forms of abuse, and are neglected—children like Freddy, Sally, and Mark from Mrs. Sorensen's class.

LIVING IN FEAR

Of all forms of abuse, domestic violence is probably the first to come to mind. Violence in the family. The images are those seen by Tanner, when his father tried to push his mother off of the front porch, or Shane when he saw his father break his mother's arm. Haunting images of betrayal. Although counter to what is now common sense, this view of men beating women tells only part of the story; women assault their spouses or boyfriends at rates about equal to or in some studies slightly higher than men assault their spouses or girlfriends.[2] Recognizing that many fathers are out of the home, mothers abuse their children at a rate approaching twice that of fathers.[3] Children also abuse other children. Regardless of the source, the results are devastating: 80 percent of men in prison were abused as children; a Sacramento study found that abused and neglected children are 67 times more likely to be arrested between the ages of 9 and 12 than other children.[4] Some children die. Happily, there is some positive news: there appears to be a decline in family violence against children and women, although not against men.[5]

In a few families, like Mark's, neglect and abuse become a way of life.

Mark

Mark, the boy in Mrs. Sorensen's class who wrote so ferociously, was late for his interview, and full of apologies despite my saying that it was all right, that I was just glad to be able to chat with him. He had to run home quickly, and he ran full speed, but he was still late and, oh, he was sorry. Polite. Considerate. Desirous to please. Mark doesn't like to disappoint adults, and he especially doesn't want to make a mistake, a mistake of any kind that will bring unwanted attention to him, that suggests somehow he isn't quite good enough or doesn't measure up to some deeply internalized and perhaps unattainable standard. Mark is hard on himself.

Mark has traveled the country a lot. He was pleased to tell me that he has been in 37 states, sometimes for more than a brief visit: 5 schools in Texas, 3 in Las Vegas, 11 total, he says. Amazing. This is the record for all the children I spoke with: 11 schools. As he talks Mark is poised, thoughtful, introspective. He likes reading, especially Mark Twain's *The Adventures of Tom Sawyer. Huck Finn* also captures his imagination. Stories of boys who are free and adventuresome; stories, it turns out, of boys very unlike Mark.

Mark's mother filled in the picture: "Mark is incredible. He really is. Mark has a lot of courage. I've yet to meet people who have more courage. He is very brave. He's very responsible. He is mature. He is thoughtful. He thinks things through. He is smart; very smart. He has great compassion. He is by nature a very kind individual. . . . Mark was born courageous." Mark's dad was a "monster. He was diagnosed as a sociopath. As you know, it is very hard to treat [such people]. . . . He was gay and come to find out he sold his body for drugs. He was a coke whore. I didn't even know this until Mark told me. I would come home from work and it was so clear that his dad was coming down from a coke high. Just so clear to me, but nothing was stolen, no drug dealers at my door asking for money, threatening to break his legs. . . . " As she spoke, I listened, saying nothing: her words flooded, gushing, rushing as though she simply had to get them out.

"I was nineteen when we got married and he was twenty-three. Well, you know we were married almost eight years, the last four years he was a coke fanatic. He was hooked on coke after our third child died. Died of crib death, even though I think I killed him. I think he suffocated him. . . . I was really young and didn't know a lot about the world, but I do now. For three and a half years he sexually abused Mark. I didn't know it until [about a year and a half ago]. He abused Mark from the time he was three and half years old to six and a half years old. There were some incidents even after I divorced him. . . . Mark never told me and I wasn't aware enough to see the signals. . . . I didn't see them. Three and a half years of living on the streets with a drug addict. I just thought Mark had a lot of bizarre behavior because it was hard and it affected him. But he was abused, severely abused." "You were on the streets?" I quickly interjected. "Yeah, we migrated everywhere. We worked from coast to coast. We lived in grungy places. I was a classic codependent. I came from a very severely dysfunctional family myself which primed me into marrying a goofball. . . . It was really bad. He was a very, very bad man." Pause. Mark's mother stared at me as though to check my reactions. Here was a natural break. I asked: "Mark displayed his courage by . . . ?" "By surviving. Not only surviving but not being a perpetrator himself. Instead of acting out the behavior which a lot of kids would do. Especially if it was steeped into such intensity. The intensity of the sexual abuse would make you vomit. I mean, it was the worst case, the worst case that [counselors] had all heard of. It was really, really, really bad. I get sick . . . with guilt. The courage to live through it. The courage to survive and not only just to survive but to redeem himself. He got dunked in a lot of manure and took a shower. It is just amazing that he is able to be who he is."

"What does that phrase mean, to redeem himself?" "Mark was dealt a really bad hand. . . . A lot of scarring. [He is] healing." Another dam broke, words flowed, cascading. "When I got pregnant two years ago, I got pregnant illegitimately, took off and here I am stuck pregnant, alone, single. So, I thought, 'you know, I really need to deal with my own sex abuse from when I was little. I need to figure out why I do the things I do. What is going on in my life. I have got to get a handle on myself.' So I started reading a book on sex abuse and Mark had all of the symptoms. I just about died. I sat down with Mark and said, 'You have all of the symptoms.' I'd been asking him for years, 'come talk to mommy if anyone tries to touch you. But you haven't talked to mommy. You haven't told me and it is time for you to tell me, and no one is going to hurt you and no one is going to kill you. Whoever said, whatever they said to shut you down so bad, is not going to happen.' Oh, my gosh, he rolled up in the fetal position, got so frigid. It was an awful summer. Then when he told me it was his dad, I almost died. . . . My brother is a marriage and family therapist, and he filed a report to the police. . . . I hate that man, [my ex].

"[Mark is bright but] three to three-and-a-half years of [abuse] every day, when he started school he was very stupid as far as the ability to concentrate, the ability to understand, the ability to follow instructions, the ability to do the work. He could not do it. He could not memorize if his life depended on it. I remember one time 30 minutes of trying to help him get the spelling word 'up,' 'up,' 'u' 'p.' He couldn't get it. He could not get anything when he went to school. I held him back in the first grade because he totally flunked out of first grade. Ds, Fs. He was a D, F student for one, two, three, four years. So what kind of message is Mark going to believe about himself? 'I'm stupid. I'm dumb . . . I can't do this.' The disclosure hit. It released Mark. You can't live for nine years and live with that kind of burden. Huge burden. When we started processing the abuse and started talking about it and started identifying it. I was stunned. . . . I just didn't think he had the capability to learn in the educational setting. Then as soon as the disclosure hit he was able to, his memory went up tenfold. I was stunned by his memory capacity after he told me about the abuse and started going into therapy and dealing with it. His grades went up. . . . It was an amazing difference."

The story was stunning. Almost unbelievable. But true. I thought of my original impression of Mark, of the eager, clean-cut student with the neatly combed short hair, raising his hand in Mrs. Sorensen's classroom and of my initial puzzlement at her suggesting I might want to talk with him. Mark is amazing, just as his mother said.

Mark's mother is grateful for the part the teachers at Lafayette have played in Mark's turnaround. He's stopped stuttering. He's completing his work. He feels safe, secure, mostly happy. Problems persist, however: he has enuresis and panic attacks, and occasional expressions of desperation, of feeling he is undeserving when good things happen to him, like a wonderful Christmas; he sometimes sabotages himself; has a fear of men; and when feeling especially depressed, makes a suicide threat. Mark's greatest fear, his mother said, is that he will "become like his father." The thought must be terrifying.

To help Mark, his mother realized she needed to straighten out her own life. No alcohol. No drugs. Therapy. Schooling to gain a career. Stable male relationships: "I have been frantically dating for a year trying to find a father for Mark. There is one guy and he seems nice and Mark likes him, [so I'm hopeful]." One of the men she dated and loved served as a positive "father figure for Mark," but the relationship didn't work out and both of them "mourned with the blues . . . Mark loved [him]. [He] loved Mark, [and that was wonderful]." She also has returned to church for her own sake, she said, and for Mark's, who, she hopes, will find positive friends and build positive relationships with men through scouting, and the young men's organization the church sponsors.

Since the discovery of abuse, Mark's mother's family has reentered her life, financially supporting Mark, his mother, and baby half-brother while she attends school and both participate in therapy. They told her, her job is to get her life together so she can help him, and she agrees. They pay for the rent on their apartment, food, and for their other needs. This is Mark and his mother's time to heal.

Like so many of the boys in his class, Mark dreams of playing in the National Basketball Association (NBA). Surprisingly, he believes with all his heart that he will have to do well in school to achieve this goal. "You have to get a lot of good scores on your tests to be able to play in the NBA." He firmly believes this is true: "You don't have to study to be an NBA player," I remarked. "Yeah you do." "Truly," I said, "you don't." "Yes you do." I heard his mother's voice in his explanation: He needs to go to college. We discussed school: "Are you a good student?" I asked Mark. "No." "You aren't? What kind of grades do you get." "I used to get F's and then I went up to B's . . . I just go up." "So, you're getting better and better?" "Yeah, now I'm on A's and B's." "So, you are a good student, then, aren't you?" Mark wouldn't grant this. Without hesitating, he said, "No."

I then tried to get him to think of himself as a student differently, and asked: "Okay, tell me why you aren't a good student." "I go too fast, like my multiplying things, I go too fast and when I read, well, I don't know about reading. I don't pay attention in class. I do all kinds of things that aren't very good." "But you know, Mark, I watch you in class. I've watched you maybe ten or fifteen times." He was amazed. "You have?!" "Yes, and you seem to me to be working hard, and your hand is up, and you ask good questions. You know, you are reading Mark Twain and a lot of kids your age couldn't read Mark Twain." "I guess," he responded, "I'm not normal." "Well, what would make you a better student?" "I guess if I'd pay attention and not rush into everything, and let some answers for other people." "And do what?" "Let answers for other people." "I don't understand." "Well, see, I'm always raising my hand and the teacher gets mad at me sometimes for raising my hand every single time." "But you raise you hand because you know the answer, right?" "Well, I think. I think I know the answer." "Isn't that what good students do?" "Yeah." "Well, are you a good student?" "I guess."

Mark loves school. Math. History. Reading. He's hungry to learn. But outside of school, he fears: fears of being abducted and fears that his mother might die: "If my mom died I would go directly to my dad. . . . He's a bad guy, he killed my little brother. . . . He abuses himself with drugs; he's a sick man. . . . I'll just tell you right now, he's a sick man." "He hurt your brother?" "Yeah, he put too much blankets on him and suffocated him. . . . His *excuse* was SIDS, but I was there and it wasn't." "That must make you feel terrible." "Mmmm-huh, he cried the whole way. I have flashbacks about that. It's hard, but I got through."

Mark prays, and prayer helps him cope with life. His prayers are answered, he said. Once, for instance, he mentioned that when he and his mother lived with some relatives he was responsible for baby-sitting five cousins. On one particularly difficult day while baby-sitting he said he "kneeled down and prayed for comfort and understanding." "Understanding of what?" "Of life, and what I am supposed to do here. I had troubles." He asked for help, for "guardian angels to come and help me through, and that's what I prayed for." He got his answer, he said, and was comforted.

Mrs. Sorensen is trying to fill in what she calls the "gaps" in Mark's schooling experience, which are considerable. For instance, it took a long time for him to begin to follow directions correctly, and he still sometimes misunderstands but she reminds him gently or reminds the entire class as a way of reminding him since he doesn't like being singled out. Many of the gaps seem to be the result of his having tuned out for so long, of not wanting to be himself as a way of softening the blows of his life with his father. In class, he works hard, and as he said sometimes too quickly. Early in the year a poor grade, often the result of having rushed through an assignment, sometimes prompted tears and guilt. His mother brought some of his papers to class upon which he had written, "I hate myself, I'm stupid," in response to having received less than a perfect grade. Since then, Mrs. Sorensen has given him the opportunity to redo his work, what she calls "do overs," which seems to help, and she monitors him closely to make certain he understands the assignment and is doing acceptable quality work. She especially avoids correcting him in front of other children, but makes a point of praising good work. Mark is making terrific progress, but the road ahead to health, to liking being who he is, as his mother said, is a long one fraught with dangers.

After the interview, I offered to take Mark home. He refused, fearing to get into a car with me. I couldn't blame him. So, intently chatting, we sauntered down the street to his apartment where his mother anxiously greeted him and vigorously interrogated me.

Chuck

Speaking softly, and avoiding eye contact, Chuck, one of Mark's classmates, says it's important for him to do well in school so he can go to college and one day play baseball. This is his dream. Despite coaching him in baseball, his father has a different dream, and wants him to be a physician. Chuck doesn't understand why, but he thinks his father has this goal for him because he "doesn't want me playing hockey or boxing." Sports matter most to Chuck, like most of the boys at school. Academics hold little interest, and Mrs. Sorensen finds that she has to constantly press him to perform, which is fine with Chuck. He expects punishment, which surprises me, so I asked, "Why is it important that [your teachers] punish you?" "Because," Chuck said with conviction, "if they didn't do that we'd be fooling around; we'd be like jumping all over the room."

Punishing students for misbehaving, Chuck says, is a sign they care. Rewards have no influence. Sadly, only punishment does.

On the surface, Chuck is quiet, unassuming. When he first entered Lafayette Elementary 2 years ago he had problems controlling his temper; he'd explode. Lately, he's mellowed, which seems to please him, and he's doing reasonably well academically, although he could do much better. But other problems have cropped up that concern Mrs. Sorensen more than academics. He is persistently late, often very late, for school. "There are days," Mrs. Sorensen remarks, "when the family doesn't wake up." He's always sleepy. I noticed he had difficulty concentrating. He is disengaged. He and his brother roam the neighborhood unsupervised, and trouble often follows, like being caught for shoplifting.

When something goes wrong in his life Chuck would rather not talk to anyone; he prefers being alone, he said. As he spoke to me, he tensed, as though this was not a topic he wanted to discuss. Calming, he opened up slightly and shared a recent troubling event, one that lingers and needs discussing, an event that prompted withdrawal: "Last week my bike messed up, so I went somewhere in a corner and just sat down [by myself]. I was riding my bike and the front tire fell off, and I thought I was going to get in trouble." "Why would you have been in trouble for that?" He paused, looking down, then volunteered, "My dad always tells me to take good care of your stuff." I didn't see the connection, so Chuck explained. He thought it was his fault the tire fell off. Someone was responsible, and it must have been him, and he expected punishment. Chuck said he worries, a lot, that he is "going to get into trouble." While he says he tries not to, he still does.

Chuck has a theory of why bad things happen, of why he gets into trouble, which he tried to explain to me in a way I would understand: cartoons. "Like on [the cartoon] Tom and Jerry, where Tom has his conscience and the little devil guy is on his shoulders. [His conscience] tells him not to do it and the little devil guy tries to get him to do it." "So, is there a devil that makes bad things happen?" "Yeah, like if you were going to do something bad and you know it is wrong, but you just couldn't help it. It is kind of hard not to." "Do you ever feel that way?" "Sometimes." "Like there is a little devil?" "Yeah." "Do you think there is a devil?" "Uh-huh. I went to two Catholic schools [and they taught] us about God and everything, like Jesus." The devil makes him do it; he wishes he wouldn't but he does.

Mrs. Sorensen has met with the father seeking his support and advice, but is suspicious of his stated good intentions since there is, she says, "no follow-through." She hasn't met the mother. Chuck and his younger brother came alone to the most recent parent-teacher conference; in fact

Chuck stayed after school to make certain he would be there on time, and despite his hunger took careful notes of what his teachers said. Mrs. Sorensen is concerned about Chuck, especially since she has noticed that nearly every day he comes to school he smells of alcohol. She has good cause for concern and is proceeding cautiously to find out what is happening at home. She suspects abuse.

Marshall, Charity, and J. B.

Three second-grade children in Mr. Lange's class share Mark and Chuck's struggles: Marshall, Charity, and J. B. J. B. lives with her mother and siblings in the recently opened battered woman's shelter, which has had a dramatic impact on Lafayette Elementary School in just the few months it has been open. Over 15 percent of the children attending the school live at this shelter, the residential drug treatment program, or in the transitional apartments for battered and homeless women and their children—three or four children on average per class—and there is a high turnover rate. J. B. hates moving.

At a distance there is a sweetness to Marshall, a charm in his smile. But he is a boy who soon wears out his welcome. In class he has great difficulty focusing and frequently is off-task, having to be reminded constantly by Mr. Lange of what he is supposed to be doing. He lags behind as other children get ready to play a math game, place-value BINGO. "Yahoo!" the children shout when Mr. Lange announces the game; it's a favorite with the children. "Marshall, do you have a card and pennies?" "No." "Come, get some." The game begins: "5460," Mr. Lange calls out. "We're looking for a five in the thousands column. If you have it, cover it [with a penny]," Mr. Lange says. Excitement grows as Mr. Lange calls out additional numbers, awaiting the first Bingo. "I GOT IT!" Marshall yells, so thrilled he can barely contain his enthusiasm. He's certain he's won. But he hasn't; he's fouled up the tens column. Marshall is into the spirit of the game, but he doesn't understand columns, one of life's great mysteries. This is as good as it gets for Marshall. He's active. He's trying to participate. He's sitting with his classmates. He's not causing problems for other children.

A "drug baby," Marshall has been diagnosed with permanent brain damage. Despite his handicap, he reads reasonably well. His mother has trouble understanding that although she has changed her life, her son will never change. The damage is done; Marshall will always have difficulty learning and controlling his behavior. Throwing Marshall's father out of the house was part of changing her life: "My mom kicked him out [cuz] he always hitted her," Marshall said. Marshall is impulsive, often "in the face" of other children; he can't sit still: he crawls around the classroom on all fours, strolls around looking for something to play with, something that he can handle even if he finds it in other children's desks, wanders quietly away from class, down the hallway or perhaps out of the school. In class he's constantly disruptive, "bouncing" around the room, as Mr. Lange kindly put it. Mr. Lange commented that Marshall had succeeded in getting the entire class upset with him; other children pull faces and try to "get away from him" as best as they can. He's right. Marshall is a child others try to avoid. Still, Mr. Lange tried to get Marshall to focus and to work in class but despite his best efforts there was little improvement as the year progressed.

Finally, Marshall's mother agreed to allow him to be evaluated by the special educator to see if he qualified for a placement in a self-contained classroom for children with severe behavioral disorders in another school. He did. But prior to testing other behaviors emerged that caused grave concern, signs of abuse: masturbating in class, "humping" little girls from behind, and commenting, "Oh, baby, that feels good," stripping naked alone in the bathroom, and peering over bathroom stalls at other children. This from an 8-year-old child! Trying to understand Marshall's behavior, a discovery was made: he had been sexually abused by an aunt. Her abuse comes on top of Marshall's other problems, of his considerable learning difficulties, difficulties that at each turn remind him of his failings, of what he can't do that other children can.

Across the room from Marshall sat Charity and J. B., a study in contrasts: Charity is freckled, blond, pale, lean, and loquacious; J. B. is dark-haired; has corn rows; and is round, reserved, and melancholy. They are friends when they aren't poking one another, calling names, or needling one another. The two as often as not work together, more rather than less productively. Charity says she and J. B. are best friends, and that she likes nothing better than to be with her, to "paint her fingernails." Mr. Lange described their relationship this way: "They would be down on each other, but they couldn't stay away from each other; kids with problems gravitate toward each other." No match made in heaven.

Charity is a reasonably good student, a bit "lazy," but one with a "good heart," as Mr. Lange said. But she has difficulty in "give-and-take" social situations, especially when she perceives that another child has something more or better than she has, even if her own possessions are sufficient—jealousy. Friendship is a possession, and Charity competes for position and possession and seeks to undermine competitors. Her greatest desire in life, she says, is to be the most "[popular] girl on earth," and to be "real cool." Cool requires having lots of things; things matter a great deal to Charity. It seems Charity will do whatever it takes to obtain her aim. Life is a soap opera, and she knows her part: catty, cruel, feigned innocence until caught. "She knows," her teacher said, "where everybody's buttons are, she knows just how to push them"; she's a "highly skilled [manipulator], . . . devilish." In group situations, she causes great difficulty and yet, her teacher said, despite her selfishness, despite her malicious teasing of other children, she has "enormous sympathy for anyone who is hurt or anyone who is in trouble. . . . She will mother anyone who is having trouble. She has great feeling. She is sensitive and emotional to the pain that someone else might be feeling."

The year before our interview, Charity's parents divorced and Charity's mother recently remarried. She and her older sister are adjusting, but not well. Girls frequently have more difficulty adjusting to remarriage than boys. "My sister worries because when [my stepfather] and my mom fight all the time, her stomach hurts. My stomach hardly ever hurts. . . . They fight all the time." "Does that make you sad?" I asked. "Uh-huh. But I don't get real scared about it, [my sister] does." "Do you worry about [your sister]?" "Uh-huh. When somebody else cries, I cry because I don't like people crying. . . . " As her teacher said, Charity has empathy. "[My stepdad] drinks," she said, "down the canyon [coming home from work] and my mom hates it. . . . [When they fight] I just pet my puppy and hide my face in it because I don't like to hear it." Charity tunes out. Life at home is tense, unhappy, uncertain. I am reminded of Tanner's life with his father. Two buried little heads hoping for silence and safety.

Charity's parents may not even be aware of her feelings, or of her sister's stomachaches, a sure sign of stress. He drinks, they fight, and the children fret.

J. B. came to Lafayette at the end of January, and was gone at the end of May, the week before the school year ended—4 months. Mr. Lange loves music, and each day the children gather around him and his piano to sing. As he gets ready to play, J. B. scoots close to him, and kneeling, places her elbows on the edge of the piano bench, rests her chin on her hands and anxiously awaits the first notes. Bright dark eyes glued firmly to Mr. Lange, she sings joyfully, robustly. This is the best time of the day, the very best for J. B. J. B.'s mother said that J. B. adores Mr. Lange and his music. Academically a good student, and often affectionate, Mr. Lange worries about J. B. because of her anger and resentment. She punishes anyone, including Mr. Lange, who attempts to correct her for inappropriate behavior, all except her mother. The anger, he said, "is always there under the surface." Her world, he sadly concluded, is in "turmoil," and she does whatever she can to hold on, to protect herself.

Like nearly all of the children I interviewed, J. B.'s is a very complicated family life. Her mother has five children, ranging in ages from 6 to

29 years old. A 14-year-old daughter lives with her father. J. B. is part of her mother's and father's second families. When we spoke, the mother, J. B., a younger brother, and older sister were living in the battered woman's shelter; before that they lived in a homeless shelter, where the mother struggled to make order in chaos. At the shelter school was held in a hallway and other mothers' children were left without direction or rules, but not hers. Her children studied.

J. B.'s mother described what happened, how she and the children ended up living in the battered woman's shelter: "We [she and her husband] had this altercation last year. I am still not ready to give up on my marriage or him. There were a lot of things going on that caused that situation to explode the way it did. To say he is a beater or batterer, I just can't say that. . . . He is going to go to anger management classes and domestic violence therapy. . . . He will be starting in a couple of weeks." "Is this a part of [the shelter's program]?" I asked. "No. They are, what they call it, they are abusers. [Men] are not allowed on the property. That is the sole reason for the family living here, [to get away from] the husband, boyfriend. They can call the police on them [if they show up here]. I don't think that is good because everyone that finds themselves in this situation, it hasn't been a lifelong thing. Some people really do change. Some people really do want to save their marriage and pull their family back together again. Then they put this great big block there." She explained that in order to see her husband, she has to "make arrangements and he usually meets us around the corner [at the grocery store or convenience store] . . . It's [hard]." The children miss their father, and want badly to live together as a family again.

One day, her husband blew up. "I had a couple of jobs when I first finished school last summer that started out paying [me] more than what he makes now [as an equipment operator] and he has been doing that for two years. To start out making more money than him . . . he's just the type of guy he really wants to be two hundred percent man in every area. [But then] my sister moved in with us and we thought and believed [she was] rehabilitated from using drugs. After she moved in we found out that she hadn't [been rehabilitated]. That caused problems. [My sister] thought he was being mean. He just was being real, and I thought he was just dumping on her, picking on her or whatever. But he was really trying to show me her. He has always said that I have been like the most naive person that he has ever known in his life. She [did terrible things] and just caused serious problems in my home and in my marriage. I always would be in her defense and he felt like I shouldn't because it was my home, our home, I am his wife, this is our family. I just wasn't seeing that, but I should have been because he was right. . . . [He blew up, finally.] I wasn't beaten. I wasn't hospitalized. I didn't have any broken bones or any disfigurement or anything. I had some bruised muscles and tissues. . . . I was in a neck brace for a few weeks. [I reported him]." She implied there had been other incidents in Michigan that led to an earlier separation yet she shoulders a large portion of blame for his actions. Many women do, and often these feelings result in reconciliations that ought to be delayed.

Her aim, above all others, is to reunite her family. "[I wish] this mess had never happened and that we were still all together as a family. I think it would make all the difference for all of our children." J. B. shares her hope. At night each of the children wish one another sweet dreams: "Have red convertible dreams and Lincoln Town Car dreams; . . . have daddy come back dreams. . . . Good daddy dreams." J. B. misses her daddy, and doesn't fully understand why they can't live together.

The husband is hesitant to return, however. J. B.'s mother's explanation of his reasoning is confusing. "He really doesn't want to do this therapy counseling thing because he thinks that any problem or any given situation he himself can work through it. . . . I feel safe enough to say that what happened last year won't [happen] again. I guess he just wants to be sure and very sure that it won't [happen]. That I won't let family come in and put a bridge between him and I. I don't know. I don't have any doubts about him wanting to reconcile the marriage and reunite the family or his love or anything like that. It is good enough for me to know that my husband absolutely loves me and I do know that and that he wants us back under the same roof again. . . . If it takes a little time to do that, then so be it. I would rather for him to have peace within himself if it took a month or three months than for us to go out this weekend and find a place to move to and move there and then he has doubts and fears. . . . I guess he is cautious." In one breath she says he is most assuredly going to get counseling; in the next he isn't, he'll take care of his feelings without help. She loves him; he loves her, that is all that matters. But it isn't.

While he contemplates getting help to manage his anger and works to support himself and to assist his wife and children, she and the children attend therapy sessions required to stay in the shelter. She doesn't like them, but she attends: "We have to go to a mandatory group every Tuesday from six-thirty to eight o'clock for adults. The ones that don't work go to school or what have you. They go Tuesday mornings from 10:00 to 11:30. The people that are in the evening group, the children go to an age-appropriate group. . . . We deal with community issues, building self-esteem. We build it, the mothers and the children as well. It is a multitude of areas and things that we cover." A taxi takes the children to school every morning. While the children are in school, the plan is for her to work at least part-time. She has three associate degrees, but "little work experience."

When the children get home from school, they do homework, chores, and Bible study 3 days a week, including a prayer and a song. The apartment is spotless, and life is carefully structured for the children. J. B.'s mother's goals for J. B. and her siblings are clear: "I want her to stay close to the Lord. I want her to stay with Christ. . . . So many changes going on every day in society and in life [I hope] that she will hold true to her family values, her Christian values and morals." In her own life, despite how difficult her situation might become, she finds support and comfort in her beliefs: "My personal relationship and belief in God, and in the Bible, [support] me." She prays that her children won't "get caught up in the wilderness, you know. Into the ways of the world. . . . Like drugs and gangs and all that. . . . We have always instilled in the children from their point of understanding, don't do a thing just because everyone else is doing it. You do what is good, what is right. . . . Make your own decisions and be responsible for your own actions, not just follow the flow."

After 4 months in the battered woman's shelter, J. B. and her family moved. Presumably the family is reunited. Hopefully, J. B.'s mother is safe and the children secure, otherwise J. B.'s deep anger most assuredly will grow and she will become increasingly difficult to teach and less likely to learn.

REFLECTIONS

Well over 3 million children are reported each year to child protective service agencies as alleged victims of child abuse and neglect, and the numbers are rising. Of these more than one third are determined to be legitimate cases, requiring action. Abused children often act out and are more aggressive than other children. Children who are abused are judged by their school peers to be "meaner and more likely to start fights and as showing less cooperation and leadership."[6] Living a profoundly lonely life in a violent family, some children "turn inward and lose contact with the outer world."[7] School performance suffers and abused children are much more likely than other children to repeat a school grade.[8] Mark, for one, had been held back.

J. B. was included in this chapter because of yet another alarming statistic: between 50 and 70 percent of men who assault their wives also abuse their children. There is a connection between spousal and child abuse; in a few families a culture of violence builds and then spreads across generations: Abused children are prone to become abusers themselves, a point not lost on Mark's mother, who fears for her son's future even as she believes he has redeemed himself. Moreover, children who witness domestic violence are at a greater risk for becoming substance abusers than are other children.

Abuse and mistreatment profoundly hurt a child's school performance; and seriously disturbed children like Marshall may also negatively affect their classmates' performance. Abuse is a problem for teachers, one they cannot avoid confronting in the classroom even if they wish to turn a blind eye. Lafayette teachers know this, and support one another in confronting it. Teachers are probably the first line of defense against abuse, although they are responsible for only between 10 and 20 percent of all reports to protective services.[9] By law all states require teachers to report suspected abuse, an action often undertaken at some personal risk to teachers. Such risk is compounded by fear that if they are wrong, if they make an honest report that proves unfounded—something always hoped for—they will only have succeeded in alienating a family and perhaps adding to a child's burdens at home. Knowing that reports are confidential eases this fear somewhat. It is only because of a teacher's concern for Marshall expressed in a grim determination to get to the truth that he is now receiving the help that he needs to begin healing emotionally and psychologically, a truth his mother sought to conceal. Such teachers are champions of children deserving praise. Marshall will never heal physically; effects of his mother's drug usage are permanent. I wonder what will happen when Marshall eventually discovers the major reason why he has difficulty learning.

Signs of abuse are often subtle and need to be understood by teachers.[10] However, one needs to make judgments cautiously, recognizing that there may be many reasons other than abuse for a change in a child's behavior that prompts concern.

CHAPTER 6

Parental Injury and Death

Death and serious injury to a parent or close relative frightens children. The finality of death, once it settles in, sometimes produces a feeling of helplessness in children, of being subjected to mysterious external forces in a capricious world. Grief "results in the loss of security of knowing that reality can be trusted to be 'real' and predictable and understandable."[1] Children respond differently to death: some become angry, as though lashing out against the unpredictability of life provides a means for overcoming fear; others feel guilt, as though somehow they are responsible for what has happened; and still others withdraw and emotionally freeze up. Fear is a basic response when a familial foundation is fractured and a child begins the struggle to reestablish identity amidst psychological and emotional upheaval made worse when the surviving parent experiences intense grief. Fear is often expressed in anxiety about the surviving parent's well-being as well as in anger, in acting out.

No one ever gets over a death, holes in the heart persist, but with help children can and do learn to accept it and go on with their lives. There is a danger, however, that adults who spend time with children will assume that because the child doesn't ask for help she is recovering nicely. Adults should know that bereavement is exhausting, and children generally don't ask for help.[2] A second danger arises from overestimating the speed with which children heal. Increasingly, it is becoming apparent that adjustment difficulties persist for a long time, although how these difficulties express themselves change over time.[3] Children need help to heal and nothing is more healing than the ability to engage in open and honest communication; ignoring suffering only increases it.

Serious injury to a parent also produces fear and anger. Family life is disrupted, relationships altered, and life made uncertain. Imagine what happens in the mind of a child when a seemingly invincible father dies or is permanently disabled; or when a mother who has stabilized life, the axis around which the family revolves, tilts, tumbles, then disappears forever. The world shatters and children spin about in uncertainty.

THE CHILDREN

Juan

For the past few months, Juan, one of Mrs. Sorensen's students, and his mother have been in hiding, the entire time he has attended Lafayette Elementary. His 29-year-old mother has been in gangs since she was 12, and her sons, including Juan, grew up believing that at some point they would gain membership for themselves, and in gaining membership would enjoy status and achieve a measure of safety for themselves and their families. One bloody evening, however, crushed her and Juan's worldview, leaving behind a fearful small boy and a mother overwhelmed with regret. Looking at his hands, Juan quietly revealed his version, one quite different from his grandmother's, of what had happened; it's a story he doesn't like to share, but he needs to share it: "My uncle was murdered in front of my house with guns." The uncle was Juan's father-figure. Now, Juan worries about dying. "They were guys, they were wearing ski masks with beanies on their heads. The [killer], he looked at me and pointed the gun at me and pointed it back to my uncle and shot it. That is when I grabbed both of my cousins, his little kids, and I threw them on the ground and jumped on top of them." "You acted like a hero," I said, more than a little surprised by the tale. Proudly: "I did good for protecting my family." He continued: "It was supposed to be a drive-by [shooting], that is where they are in a car and they just roll down the windows and shoot at people. They were supposed to do a drive-by at some gangsters, and they . . . just shot when [my uncle] was outside with his girlfriend. The girl, his girlfriend, just got shot in the leg. Now she has a metal thingy as her knee and down her leg that connects to her foot." Juan was traumatized, and in the story I found an answer to the principal's question posed before we spoke: "If you can gain any insight into why Juan is so angry, I'd appreciate it." Juan is constantly on guard, and he fantasizes heroism. When his uncle was murdered he and his cousins were inside the house, his grandmother claims, having been sent there by the uncle who saw danger coming.

Following the murder, Juan's mother "went on a four-month drunk," as she described it, after which sobering thoughts settled in. "When I stopped drinking," she said, "all I kept thinking was, 'my brother is gone, and for what?' I had a son with problems. Juan saw the whole thing happen. He had problems sleeping at night after that. I just said, 'that is it, I've had enough.' I moved away. I moved away. Me and him moved. . . . It was too much chaos in that house. My family is into the gangs so I just decided that I am getting the hell out and I did. I got the hell out and got Juan out of there. A month and a half later my mom came, and she has been with me since. My mom didn't live with my dad for almost ten years. They had been separated and when my brother was murdered she moved back in with him. It still wasn't working." She took Juan with her into hiding, but not her other two sons who have a different father, a gangster. Juan's father, also a gangster, lives with another woman and has two additional sons, future soldiers.

She has regrets, lots of regrets. Quietly, as though speaking to herself, Juan's mother muses, "The way I have lived has gotten me nothing." Since fleeing her old neighborhood, with the encouragement of Lafayette's special education teacher, she enrolled in evening courses to receive her GED. She said that Juan was a major reason for her doing this: "I am trying to show Juan that if I work hard at something, then he needs to do the same thing. This is new for me, and it is new for him. I don't know how to do this, I know how to live a rotten life. I don't know how to live a good life," and she struggles each day to think ahead, to think about a future she had never thought of before, having only been concerned with the day, perhaps yesterday, but never tomorrow. Doubts haunt her. She openly wonders if the changes she has made have come too late.

Juan's mother spoke sadly of her brother's six children, how they had been placed in "separate foster homes" because the mother is a drug addict. She laments that her brother was killed just as he seemed to be getting his life straightened out. He stopped using drugs, she said, and the future looked a bit brighter for him and for his three youngest children, all girls. There was hope, but quickly her feelings of regret return: "I just want Juan to know there is better things out there. . . . [I wish] I just would have been a better mom. . . . I was a very young mom and I didn't have hardly any brains. I [should] have stayed in school and do what I was supposed to be doing and I would be able to provide a lot better for him. [And] I wouldn't have raised him in the neighborhood that he was raised in. . . . There are a lot of kids out there that ain't got a chance. I think that there are a lot of kids that I know that could be something . . . but they never will because they don't have the opportunities. Everyone says, you know, to look at your parents who will guide you and half of them kids out there ain't got no parents. Their parents are high on drugs, and they don't have anyone to fall on except themselves and the first place that they hit is the gangs, and that is where it all starts. A lot of them kids are going to find themselves dead or in prison and I am hoping that Juan can look back on this and just thank God that he didn't make them decisions."

Still, she is fearful. Juan *is* angry, and not only his teachers see it. To help him deal with his trauma, the special education teacher invited his grandmother and mother to make a presentation for other children on gangs and violence, which seemed to help the family heal. Still, Juan is often abusive toward his mother and grandmother, the latter who supports the family working at a warehouse; and he is increasingly difficult to control. "I have totally changed my life around for this kid, and sometimes it is just like I didn't do enough and that worries me." She hopes others will give Juan a chance: "People . . . see gang members as just kids that ain't got a heart and they don't look at them as individual people." She wanted others to see the goodness in her son that she sees, but at times even she has difficulty recognizing it.

In school Juan's anger expresses itself in occasionally frightening ways. He has "attitude," and makes up for his diminutive size by posturing, swaggering, and by aggressiveness, which he sincerely believes others admire. As Mrs. Sorensen remarks, "He steals. He lies. He swears at kids. He likes looking tough. He likes being in charge. He is sexually knowledgeable," even going so far as to threaten one of his classmates by telling her he and a friend ought to "pull her pants down and rape her." He charms girls, but then turns mean and frightening. His world is a female world—teachers, the principal, his mother and grandmother— and at times he demonstrates resentment. Mrs. Sorensen doesn't like Juan's attitude, and doesn't trust him, knowing that whenever her back is turned he is likely getting into trouble. She feels she has failed. "I feel like [he behaves] just out of fear of me and my punishments. . . . I don't like that. It makes me feel bad, if you want to know the truth."

Others see subtle changes in Juan; a little less aggressiveness shown on the playground toward other children, a little more honesty, and a little more openness. Juan sees changes in himself: he is in far fewer fights than he was in his previous school, and proudly reports that he is doing more homework and that his grades are better than they have ever been. In part, he attributes these changes to feeling, for the first time in his life, safe at school. His mother notes changes as well: he reads better, she said, and he brings home his daily planner so she can make certain he does his homework. He's made terrific progress in mathematics, now being slightly above grade level.

It is on the football field where Juan seems free, when his anger is channeled, his fears lifted, and where his poor reading ability has no bearing on his peer status. Other children know he's a good player, quick, agile, skilled; and they admire his play. He dreams of being a Denver Bronco, and watching him on the playground, it is easy to imagine him breaking tackles, catching or deflecting passes, and running away from a defender, perhaps with the same determination and intensity his mother shows in trying to escape her past in the hope of creating for Juan a different and better future.

Vincente

Vincente is in second grade. During place-value BINGO—mentioned in the previous chapter—Vincente sat outside the student group that surrounded Mr. Lange, his teacher, as he called out numbers and awaited the first "Bingo!" Leaning back against a table, Vincente looked in at the action of the group until Mr. Lange invited his participation. In response, Vincente, who looked like he'd dressed hurriedly that morning in his wrinkled red plaid shirt and Levis, scooted across the carpet on his bottom and moved to the outer edge of the group, not in, not out, and began playing. He even won a game. "Winners get one dip into the good stuff [the caramel popcorn jar]," Mr. Lange announced. Vincente smiled broadly. At game's end, many grubby hands plunged into the jar, and stuffed sticky brown popcorn into smiling, chattering faces.

Although he is doing better, for 4 months Vincente has been very angry, and distant—often on the fringes of class activity. For a time Mr. Lange wondered if Vincente could stay in class: "There were one or two times when I didn't feel like Vincente could really be in class. He couldn't follow any kind of instructions. I took him to the office, [not so much as punishment] but to give him a little time and a little space.... The anger seems to be under better control now.... There is still that initial tendency to bang into the world ... but it isn't as severe. [No more] full-blown battles.... I haven't seen him be hysterical in a long time."

Seven-year-old Vincente's world collapsed when his father, his best friend, favorite playmate, soccer coach, and cycling companion, was crushed by a falling wall at a construction site when supports gave way. "I am the closest to my dad as I can get," Vincente said. At first, physicians thought the father would most certainly die, but he didn't; he was in a coma for weeks, and now lives with severe brain damage. Just prior to the accident, Vincente had been moved into a higher mathematics class, but 3 weeks later he lost motivation and the ability to concentrate. His teachers asked if he could be moved down a level where he would be under less pressure to perform. He wasn't keeping up. He was elsewhere—in the hospital, mentally, with his father. As his mother remarked, the accident "threw him off balance, and just made lots of things unimportant to him." She was aware of his anger: "He had some outbursts at school, and I have had him in counseling since the accident. The last session he had was a couple of weeks ago and the counselor said that she thinks Vincente is a wonderful kid, and has adjusted well. The first couple of sessions she was worried."

Every day Vincente and his three siblings visit the hospital with their mother. After school, his mother, a shy, dark, delicately beautiful young woman, picks him up. They go home and have dinner, he does homework, and by 6:30 or 7:00 the whole family travels to the hospital to sit with the father, where she has spent most of the day. I interviewed her there, in the lobby, which has become a kind of home away from home. She knows precisely what Vincente and his siblings are experiencing since her own father died in an accident when she was a child. Her mother, who raised five children on her own, provides much of the support she and the children need: "She has been there for me the whole time. She picks them up for me in the morning, takes them to school, brings them breakfast. She baby-sits for me all day Saturday and Sunday after church. She spends a lot of time with them. My husband and I have struggled financially and she helps buy them clothes, and she teaches them Spanish. She is amazing."

Vincente's is a close and loving family, a family whose members are dedicated to one another's health and happiness. In addition to her mother, Vincente's family finds support in their Mormon congregation, their "ward." "My neighbors and ward members are just wonderful," Vincente's mother said. "They are extremely supportive. They watch my kids for me. . . . They have been up to see Vincente's father. They [conducted] a fast. . . . He spoke on Thursday. Wednesday the doctor came in and told me that he had done another EEG and Vincente's father was only one step up from brain dead. He had only primitive brain functions and that was as good as it got. That was Wednesday. We were only here [in the rehabilitation center] on a trial basis. I asked the doctor to please give him a chance, and they did. We were here for about three weeks and they said this was going to be the last week because he just didn't respond and they didn't think there was anything to work with. The next day . . . he spoke." She continued, slowly, thoughtfully, sharing a sacred moment for her and for her family: "We asked the ward to fast and pray that he would make some kind of progress. . . . Thursday he spoke; he remembered and he answered questions. Once he did that, he started following commands and trying to roll over, raise his arms, closing his eyes. He is doing all of it. He is laughing. He is making jokes." Supposedly, none of this is medically possible for the father. Physicians are astonished. For Vincente's mother, these improvements in her husband's condition confirm her faith. She expresses gratitude that she and her husband "haven't left things unsaid, or undone. We are just close. I figured I would rely on his strength, his faith and my faith [to get through this]."

At home, Vincente misses his father, and prefers being at the hospital to being anywhere else. When he gets home from the hospital, he said, "I lay in bed and think of my dad and try to fall asleep." He says he's tired a lot, and all he wants to do is sleep. At school, at home, at the hospital, his thoughts are the same, always about his dad. Vincente says that school has become more difficult since the accident, and that he has changed. His anger especially concerns him: "I get angry out of control. I was never like this. Now, when I am angry I go up into my room and start throwing stuff at the walls. I try not to but it feels like I just have to." He prays: "I pray tons. When I wake up, before I come to school, and before I go to bed. I pray for my dad that he would get better every day. . . . I prayed one time that he would talk, and it is answered, he's talking."

Like his mother, he takes strength from his religious community: "Our ward, we are like brothers and sisters. [We call each other] brother and sister. . . . " I asked, "Is that a good thing to be called brother and sister?" "Yeah, it makes me think that I have a family across the world. That helps me. . . . Me and my friend from our ward, we prayed that [my dad] would talk and it came true."[4] Vincente is a boy with tremendous faith, but also one facing a tremendous trial: "I only have one worry," he said, "that my dad won't live and that is the only worry that I have. But I know he is, so I don't have any fears of the future. I don't have any." Despite his remarkable faith, Vincente is a boy suffering, a boy whose world has been flipped upside down, who finds himself struggling in school to engage in activities that have lost their meaning, and who has only one concern, a wish: "I wish for my dad to be alive forever."

Bart

Bart, a sixth-grade student, was hard to miss. For days I sat in the back of Mr. DeCourse's room and watched Bart, a perfectly oval child from any and all angles, top, back, side, rear, standing by his seat near the doorway and gazing blankly out the window. He'd sit, say nothing; expressionless, he'd look around but not at anything in particular. Sometimes while sitting at his table he'd fiddle with his backpack, cut paper with scissors seeming to work on an assigned project, or absentmindedly thumb through a book and look at a picture. Mostly he would sit quietly, or stand gazing. "Bart, don't you have anything to do?" Mr. DeCourse would occasionally ask. In response, Bart would get busy for a short time. While listening to the *Phantom of the Opera* one day, Bart asked a question. He wondered, "How [does] putting a hand in front of the face prevent death from the Magic Lasso?" Mr. DeCourse showed him how. Listening to Bart's question, I wondered if he was thinking about his mother, who died just a few days before Christmas.

When I asked Bart if we could talk, he didn't look up. He never looked at me; he blushed, backed up, turned, and silently shuffled away down the hall. By speaking to him, I almost felt ashamed, as though I'd intruded into a place I didn't belong and had no business being. Immediately I knew Bart would not be interviewed, but I still unobtrusively observed him in class. I asked Mr. DeCourse if there were ways in which I might help Bart, who seemed so very, very far away, so deeply depressed.

While his mother was ill, and she was ill for an extended period of time, Bart was angry and threw tantrums. Realizing Bart wasn't getting counseling, Mr. DeCourse became concerned. After his mother's death Bart's behavior worsened for a time and Mr. DeCourse spoke with the principal about what he should do: "I have never had such a tough case—passive, resistive, angry, tough kid." The principal encouraged Mr. DeCourse to give Bart time and space. He did. Some assistance came from the part-time school counselor who made an effort to periodically visit with Bart. When I met Bart, he had closed down emotionally. He needed to talk about his feelings, certainly, but not with me, who he saw as an intruder instead of a friend and trusted adult. Mr. DeCourse gave him space, resisted pressing him too much about completing his school-work, encouraged him in class and supported him, was available to chat, and waited patiently for Bart to complete his mourning. In time, he began to shows signs of healing. For a time, school was placed on hold.

Mapa

Mapa is 8 years old—a giant of a child, but gentle, talkative, and quick to smile, like his father who was a dear friend of mine for many years. December 10 was the worst day of Mapa's life, but it didn't begin that way. He had a wonderful time at his family's party. All the uncles and aunts and cousins were there, dozens and dozens of them. He was very happy. Early that evening Mapa's dad danced a Tongan war dance, yelping and grinning broadly all the while as he cajoled his daughters and some of the cousins to join in. Sheepishly, some did to the delight and pleasure of all attending. The dance was videotaped, and Mapa's mother and I watched it together. This was a profound act of generosity on her part, one I shall never forget. When the music ended, Mapa Sr. acknowledged the cheering crowd and immediately began searching for his children to see if any of them wanted to leave the party to go home with him to help prepare for his wife's return flight from California later that night. Mapa loved being with his father so he and one of his sisters went with him. Mapa's mother had been visiting her parents. At home, Mapa's father sat down on the living room couch to rest for a moment. A few minutes later he cried out his son's name. Mapa rushed to his father's side just as he slipped into coma and died from a massive heart attack. Forty-eight years old, powerfully built and athletic, no one, including me, imagined he would ever die. To Mapa, his father was invincible. Late that night two uncles met Mapa's mother at the airport and took her directly to the hospital where, as she walked unsteadily into the emergency room, she saw her husband stretched out on a gurney, gray and lifeless. As she entered the harshly lighted room the circle of women surrounding Mapa's father's body parted, making way for her to kiss, touch, and caress her lifeless husband. Women wailed; men stood silently around the outer walls of the room, tears trickling down many of their faces. Grief-stricken, an uncle fainted and crumbled to the floor. Children sobbed. A cousin and two daughters stroked Mapa's father's thick, black, wavy hair, crying, pleading with him to return. I know this because I was there standing with the men.

Mapa is the youngest of seven children, five sisters and an older brother in his 20s who lives away from home. A beloved adopted child, Mapa went everywhere with his father, a leading figure in the Tongan community, a man noted for his generosity and goodness. Three funeral services were held for Mapa Sr.: One for the family; one in Tongan; and one in English, a Mormon service. Mapa's family is deeply dedicated to their faith and believe in an afterlife where families are reunited forever. The thought is comforting. Mapa's father held an important position within the local religious congregation, and was quick to give service to others in need. The entire community grieved his loss. At the funerals the children spoke, including Mapa, and sang magnificent melodic tributes to their father who loved to sing as well as to dance. Mrs. Novakovich, Mapa's third-grade teacher who is also a close friend of the family, attended the services, provided a meal, and as is the "Tongan way," gave money to the family. His classmates wrote cards for Mapa expressing their sadness about his father's death. Mapa's grandfather, who has serious health problems of his own, and his grandmother, his mother's parents, quickly made plans to move in with the family to support their daughter and the children in their time of grief.

Returning to school was difficult for Mapa. He tried to concentrate, but sometimes couldn't. He wanted to be home with his family. Mapa's a very good student, although it sometimes amazes Mrs. Novakovich that he is able to get his work done since he talks incessantly. "Mapa is very social, loves everybody, wants to talk all the time," she said. "An incredible thing about Mapa is that he is one of the few students that can talk from the minute he comes into the room to the moment he leaves and still accomplish all of the assignments he is given. The only problem is that all of the children at all of these tables [around him] can't work [with him talking]." Mapa said he wants to do well in school because "my mom wants me to work hard [and] for my dad." At home, he and his mother read together almost daily: "Yes, he is a good student," his mother said. "In reading, he come to me and I said, 'I could help you but you know reading.' He kind of helped me out, too, pronounce words. I don't know pronounce compound words, those long words, right. He kind of help me sound it out. He knows that I don't speak the language very good."

With his father, a crew leader in a large bakery, Mapa enjoyed working on cars and speculates that he might do this for a living, but he also thinks seriously about becoming a teacher like Mrs. Novakovich. He isn't certain. What he is certain about is that he wants to give honor to his father and to his mother. He spoke of his father: "I always wanted to be like my dad, so I act like him." His mother shares his dream, and more: "I want him first to be just like his dad. I want him to be well educated, better than me and his father. I want him to have a good life that he can depend on him, and his family to depend on him."

Like so many other children who experience death of a parent or abandonment, Mapa has one worry: "Well, my worry is that I'd hate to see my mom die."[5] The death of his father terrified him. Exhausted, Mapa had a dream in the hospital where he dozed briefly while a prayer was being said over his father's body: "When we went to the hospital and they told me that my dad was dead, when we were saying a prayer, I closed my eyes and I was listening to the prayer, too, and I found like a little place [where I went]. It scared me. We sat like in these chairs and we like go and we would get up and talk and then somebody [got up] and kissed my mom's cheek and sang an Italian song. Then it was my turn to get up. It shocked me when I saw my mom lying in there, [dead]." He went on to explain his fears: "I was crying at the funeral. I was trying to get rid of the dream. I was up by the coffin [his dad's coffin]."

Back at school, Mapa had difficult moments. "What do you do when you feel sad, Mapa?" "[Mrs. Novakovich] showed me a place where I can go. I can close the door, cry and feel sad for a while and come out. . . . It helped me a lot. Somebody was making fun of me. Can I say, well, I told my sister that this guy, this boy called me a jerk and was rude and then I didn't do anything. He was saying, 'Dead Dad.'" "He said what?" I asked in disbelief. "Dead dad. It made me cry. He was making fun of me and stuff. . . . I went to my place." Mrs. Novakovich described what happened: "One time he asked if he could go to the rest room and while he was in the rest room, it hit him. Some boys came to me and told me that he was in the rest room crying. I went and got him and had a talk with him. I think he went to the rest room because he felt he could go there and remove himself from the class and go cry and other kids wouldn't see and be worried. The bathroom wasn't an option, either. Too many other kids would come in and out of there. So we made arrangements for him to have a spot. There is a little sick room that is in the office. We made arrangements for him to be able to go in there if he felt like he needed some time. He didn't use it that often. . . . He would come to me and ask, 'Can I go to my place?' I'd say, 'Yep,' and he'd just go there. He has lots of friends. The kids care about him. . . . The kids were very sad and sorry for him. A couple of them have had parents, dads, die."

He also prays when he feels bad: "I say prayers on my own that I might feel good. Most of the time I wish I can die so that I can be with my dad, but it wouldn't happen until I am older. . . . " We spoke of his feelings: "You know," I said, "if you were to leave, think how sad we would all be, it would break [many people's] hearts." "Well . . . I wish for it a lot." "Whose name do you have?" I asked. "My dad's name, my brother's name, my dad's dad's name." "And what does that say about the importance of you staying here?" "To take on the name and pass it on," he said. "And bring honor to it, right? Isn't that the Tongan way?" "Yeah." More than anything in his life, Mapa wants his father back, but he still senses his presence: "I feel his spirit in me," he said, quietly, reverentially.

With his father dead, Mapa's mother worries about his future. She is especially concerned about gangs. Her older son was pressured to join, and now she worries that Mapa will also be pressured, but unlike his older brother he won't have the steady and strong arm of his father to help him resist. In the meantime, he has his special place in the school where he can go to grieve.

Dylan

Dylan was also in Mrs. Novakovich's class. When Dylan was 3, his father died of cancer, yet he recalls being with his father, being loved and being happy. Mrs. Novakovich worries about Dylan: "He is a very bright little boy but I have to stay on him all the time to get any project done. Sometimes he just doesn't get things finished. He is such a sad, very depressed little boy. . . . He is very, very bright. He is probably one of the best readers I have in the classroom. Obviously he knows a lot of things . . . I've always felt Dylan was carrying some weight [around]. Something that makes him so sad that he just can't cope with things. He cries easily if something is real frustrating to him. If somebody starts [trouble] . . . he starts to cry. Sobs uncontrollably. I have to settle him down. Usually it is something that another child starts but he will not tattle on them. He will never tell on them even if it means that he would be off the hook and they would be in trouble. There is just such a deep sadness about him. It's hard to put a finger on it. I don't think lots of times he can get beyond whatever is going on in him internally—to really work and do the work he needs to do." Dylan almost never smiles. Rarely does he interact with other children. Mrs. Novakovich loves him and tries to show him that she cares for him. He believes her when she says he is smart: "Are you a good student?" I asked. "Yeah." "What makes you a good student?" "That I am smart and I always listen." "How do you know you are smart?" "Because my teacher always tells me." "And you believe her?" "Yeah."

Dylan is lonely. There are not many children living near his apartment, and he wishes he had more friends. "I pray that I would have a lot more friends because there are very few kids in this neighborhood." When asked what would make him most happy, Dylan didn't hesitate: "To see my dad again. . . . I can't remember what he looked like; he was always nice. It would be a happy moment." He explained that his dad "is in heaven" and that he looks forward to seeing him. Dylan is troubled that his mother is remarrying, a man who fathered his sister, and that in preparation for moving out of the area, pictures of his father have been put away where he cannot get to them. For now, he longs for his father, plays outside after school until it is late, well past dark, looks forward to when the apricots on the tree near his apartment will ripen, and anticipates the next day with pleasure, spending time in the school library, his favorite place of all places to be.

Tommy

Tommy, Sally's brother from Mrs. Sorensen's room, was also in Mrs. Novakovich's class. Tommy spent a great deal of time in Mrs. Novakovich's room before and after school. He liked it there, and enjoyed the abundance of interesting things around her room—stuffed animals, Madagascar roaches, rats, spiders, music to play, a huge cardboard box made into a boxcar, lots of books (mostly her own), and fun artwork. While there, bouncing from item to item—Tommy can't sit still—he chatters, and sometimes helps her get ready for the next day's class. He liked helping and talking. One day while jabbering, he told Mrs. Novakovich that his father was dead. She believed him. Recall, Sally and Tommy's mother wasn't certain what had happened to her former husband, but to

Tommy she said he was dead. Telling him this ended all speculation. It was a seemingly simple solution to a knotty problem, a problem she apparently didn't want to face herself, or didn't want Tommy to have to face. Her solution was a bit like not telling Sally that she knew about the violin lessons. Some things are better not said, not known. Like Little Dan, Tommy didn't grieve; one can't grieve for something never known. Yet he still sensed that he had missed out on something of value. Maybe life would have been better had his father lived: his death, for Tommy, is but another reminder, among many, that life is precarious.

REFLECTIONS

Mourning is "giving up one's attachment to a loved one, [and] is a slow and arduous and exhausting task."[6] But before mourning can begin children must understand and accept the death of a loved one. Losing a parent means losing a part of oneself and it is the surviving parent who, despite grieving, must help the child accept death.[7] Once mourning begins, teachers have a role to play. To help a child they need to understand that mourning never ends; life events may trigger a return of feelings of loss, and the teacher needs to respond. Some children, a significant minority, even show serious behavioral problems a year or two after the parent's death.[8]

There is a rough pattern to grieving. In the first few weeks following a death, children will regress and engage in behaviors that adults think have been outgrown. Anxiety at bed time, nightmares, fear of leaving home, difficulty sleeping, fatigue and mood swings. The child may miss school because of physical complaints and when in class act in uncharacteristic ways. Children may worry about illnesses, overreact and imagine they are about to die. To be sure, sometimes they are ill; stress produces a variety of ailments.[9] Anger, guilt, and depression are common expressions of the child's anxiety. Over time, most children adjust to an environment without their parent and they begin to resituate the dead parent within their emotional lives.[10] As they do so, they begin to be more like themselves.

When I first met Bart he had withdrawn deep into himself. He was grieving, but not yet mourning. As I write, both he and Mapa seem to be healing. Mapa still shows occasional signs of depression, but they are less and less frequent, and he says he doesn't need to go to his "place" anymore. In contrast, Vincente grieves still. Despite the progress his father has made, he is not the father Vincente knew; he will never coach soccer again nor ride bikes with his son. Recognizing that she must fully support the family, his mother is back in school—more disruption. Unlike Bart and Mapa, Vincente cannot yet move on, cannot heal. It has been a year since his father's accident, and he still has difficulty concentrating in class. He is less angry, but he continues to struggle with his emotions. His father will live, as he hoped and prayed, but nothing is as it was.

As families reel from death or severe injury to a parent, children need more than ever to be assured that they are loved, that adults, like their teachers, are willing to listen to their expressions of sadness and loss and help them get reoriented. Families need to know that teachers will help, like Mrs. Novakovich when she visited Mapa's family, brought a meal, and attended the funeral services. Children also need support from their classmates, who typically do not know how to respond appropriately and helpfully to death. The sympathy cards Mapa's classmates made for him deeply touched Mapa, eased his return to school, and helped him to heal. They also comforted his mother, who worried about each of her children and how they would cope with their father's death. Making the cards gave Mrs. Novakovich an opportunity to talk with the children about death and to reassure them. Some had pets that had died, and these experiences helped them better grasp what Mapa was feeling so they could comfort him when he returned. Dylan, especially, understood something about the hole Mapa feels. Unfortunately, few teachers feel they are qualified to deal with death issues, but they must.[11] The worst action an adult can take is to ignore the child and avoid the issue.

Children heal in their homes. Obviously some homes are more healing than others. But teachers can help. Each of the Lafayette teachers sought to support the children, looking forward to when they would again be engaged actively in the classroom. They gave time to heal, but they also thoughtfully nudged them along as much as they could toward fuller classroom participation. "Bart, don't you have anything to do?" was Mr. DeCourse's way of telling Bart that at some point he would need once again to get serious about his studies. And he did. At the year's end Mr. DeCourse said he wrote a "terrific report on Scotland." Mr. DeCourse was thrilled. Bart was beginning to move on with his life.

CHAPTER 7

Family Instability

The preceding chapters address several life circumstances that contribute to family instability: poverty and the need to move frequently, ever in search of affordable housing; divorce, sometimes leading to what can best be described as serial polygamy; the absence of a father and mothers who have multiple partners; drug abuse; movement into and out of foster care; and parental injury and death. While family instability is a symptom with many causes, its effects are far-reaching for children. Children whose lives are unstable have difficulty trusting anyone or anything. They want to trust others, they desperately want to love and be loved, but often do not know how to trust or to love. The lesson many children learn is straightforward and disturbing: When life is unpredictable, it is best to take care of oneself and to avoid investing heavily in others who are certain to disappoint. Brad and Freddy from Mrs. Sorensen's class are two such children.

THE CHILDREN

Brad

With head resting on his hands, Brad, from Mrs. Sorensen's class, looked puzzled when I asked how many brothers and sisters he had—a seemingly simple question, I thought, but I was wrong. He scrunched his face, paused, pushed back in his chair, pursed his lips, rolled his sparkling dark eyes, and began counting on his fingers slowly, deliberately, then said, "let's see, hmmm, six." "Six?" "Wait, seven." "Seven?" "Wait, eight." "That's a hard question." It wasn't meant to be. "I didn't count [two] sisters." "Oh." Brad explained, "My dad was married to four different ladies and has had quite a few kids." Brad had a hard time remembering when he last saw these two siblings, who are older and live in other states. Even with his best effort, he was off one child, according to his stepmother.

I met Brad for the first time just before Mrs. Sorensen's class left for the computer lab. I followed the line of exiting children and once in the lab helped some with their writing. When the lab session was over, the children lined up by the door to leave. Standing in line, Brad, scrubbed and sparkling clean, looked up at me and directly into my eyes, moved so he was standing right in front of me, smiled broadly and without blinking asked for a hug. This was a new experience. I smiled back and pulled him to me. My reaction to Brad's request seemed natural, proper. He beamed, we parted, and the line moved out toward Mrs. Sorensen's room. Suddenly we were friends.

Brad has moved around a lot, having attended five different schools, but he is settled now with his father in his stepmother's home. The new marriage is stable, his parents say, and life for Brad is more predictable than it has ever been, but life remains complicated: Through this latest marriage, Brad gained yet another brother and another sister, and he lives in their house, in his 21-year-old stepbrother's room.

For the first time in Brad's life he has a mother who sets and reinforces rules. The house is orderly, and Brad is expected to do his part. He cleans and follows the established rules, including asking permission before watching television. This is a new and different rule for Brad, one he isn't certain he likes. But he knows that in his stepmother's house, breaking rules brings consequences.

Having nearly finished raising her own children, it's difficult for Brad's stepmother to face the challenge of raising yet another child, let alone two, but when she married Brad's father she resolved to do all that she could to help Brad, as she put it, "be the kind of person that he needs to be." She appears to be a determined woman, one not used to failing. "I think he is capable. I think he has a good personality. I think he is very bright, and I think he knows the answers [adults] want to hear. . . . [But, he is a thief] right now. We don't know why he steals, but he does and he is going to go to court for it. . . . We have got to change this desire in him before it gets too late, before he is older." She not only worries about Brad, however. She worries that her husband's children are so demanding that their marriage is being hurt.[1] "We need time to be a couple." She feels some resentment, and then guilt: "By the time I raise these kids I will be old, and then I'll die."

Brad lowered his voice and said, "I steal." His behavior puzzles him. He doesn't understand why he steals; and he wishes he knew why. And he worries. "My parents tell me that if I keep on taking things that I might grow up to be a thief. . . . I take things. It started when I was in third grade, and I have no idea how many times [I've stolen]. Lots." "What happens when you get caught?" "I get into trouble, big trouble." "Why do you keep taking things, then?" "I don't know. I haven't the slightest idea. . . . I like money so I took my [older] brother's twenty-one dollars." "But you said you didn't need it." "I didn't need it, but I like money for some reason." "Did you spend the money?" I asked. "No." "Brad, what's wrong with being a thief?" "You get thrown into jail." "Do you feel bad when you take things?" "Yeah. It has become like a kind of habit." "What do you mean, that it is a habit?" "I know I can stop it, but it is really hard to stop." "Do people feel badly when you take things?" "Yeah." "How does that make you feel?" "Bad that somebody else is feeling bad because of me." "You worry that maybe your parents are right, that you are a thief?" "Yeah." "Do you think about jail?" "Yeah . . . I go to [the Children's Center for counseling] and they have this time-out place and it is a lot like jail. You sit in this room. Nothing is there but windows [he sighs]. No escape." "Do they lock you in?" I asked. "Yes." Brad then described his experience with counselors and in family therapy. Despite his parents' and counselor's best efforts, Brad still steals, and he frets about his future. Maybe, just maybe, he is a thief, he fears, no matter what. He's fated. Yet when this boy who worries about being sent to jail is asked what would make him most happy if he were given one wish, he smiled and said, "To see for myself if there is really a Santa Claus or not." His sister thought there wasn't, but he was uncertain, desperately hoping she was wrong.

Shortly after this interview, Brad was caught stealing again. He broke into a vending machine while attending an after-school program while his parents were working. In response to this latest incident, Brad's parents decided that he should enter the juvenile justice system in the hope that he might begin to take responsibility for his actions, to try to change what seems to Brad in one breath to be fate, his having been condemned to be a thief, and in another breath a matter of his having chosen to do wrong. In either case, he feels he is a playing field for evil, and he doesn't understand why. Despite constant and consistent counseling and parental admonitions, he doesn't change. His stepmother seems to hold a view similar to his, which troubles her deeply: "I know that he knows what is right. It is not a matter of not knowing, it is just something in him that he [steals]. I don't know." Brad doesn't know, either; confused and hopeless, at times he threatens suicide.

Brad's natural mother is a drug addict who was ordered by the court not to see him again; she was to have no involvement in his life whatsoever. The mother is a "tramp," his stepmother asserts, and much worse. Tensing, she says that the mother allowed Brad and his sister to be sexually abused, and participated in the abuse. The details are sketchy, the damage is deep, but the evidence, she said, is compelling. Despite being mistreated, both children still wonder why their mother rejected them: What was wrong with them? Brad, his stepmother laments, lacks basic trust and she "can't give it to him." She explains, "I didn't get them when they were little babies to teach them." Still, despite constant disappointment, she remains determined. She knows there are no quick fixes.

In yet another attempt to find ways of reaching Brad, she and her husband enrolled in a parenting class. While they were in class one evening, Brad stole some candy, but when confronted by his stepmother, denied it: "No, Mom," he said, "honest, [a boy] gave it to me." Which was untrue. More stress; more disappointment; more punishment. "I don't believe anything Brad tells me," she said, but she badly wants to. "That is a real hard thing for a child to know that your parents don't believe you, neither one of us do. . . . I like to trust him, [but I can't]." As I listened, I was glad I'd hugged Brad and he hugged me.

Despite his troubles, Brad was near the top of Mrs. Sorensen's class academically. He has very high standardized test scores, the kind of scores that swell parents prone to bragging. He reads well above grade level, perhaps 2 or 3 years above, writes well and, according to Mrs. Sorensen, he "catches deeper meaning" in events and stories that most other children do not. "I think that comes from his own life experiences. He is able to fill in some of the literature we've been reading this year," she said. "For example, like *Number the Stars* and *Feeling of Fear*. A question was asked: 'Do you think World War Two would leave scars on Anna Marie and Ellen and her family?' Brad was the only child who responded in a thorough way. He said, 'Yes, because when you lose people or people die or they leave you, it leaves horrible scars. I know because my mother left me when I was four.' . . . He feels [deeply], and he can put that feeling into his writing." Brad knows he's smart, which makes his behavior even more puzzling to the adults who care about him.

Mrs. Sorensen worries "a lot" about Brad. "I worry about his stealing and his lying. I really worry. [He's heard voices] this year; he hears voices. Personally, I think that was stress because he had that court hearing [at the same time this was going on]. It was the first time he had to face police action for his stealing. I think it was wise on his mother's part and the counselor's part to [follow through in this way]. That needed to happen. . . . But I really worry about him." She went on to report that the voices stopped once he completed his court-ordered community service. The voices terrified Brad and frightened Mrs. Sorensen, who recalls him walking toward her during class stopping and standing silently before her, a fragile small boy, ghostly white, seemingly ill. Then he told her about the voices. The voices. Mrs. Sorensen, the rock, tucked away her own fears, succeeded in calming his, and later contacted his stepmother to tell her what had happened and to share her concerns.

In addition to his stepmother, Brad knows that he can count on Mrs. Sorensen. When she sets a rule, she means business! "He banks on it," she says. "Still, just as any child waits for me to remind him it is Friday, and he still owes me work, I keep him in [from recess]. I keep him because of his guilt, [and of his need to meet with me]. I keep him because he is happier when I do." Brad needs high levels of structure in class, and she gives it to him. She faithfully follows through with him, making certain he completes his assignments and that each day he has accurately recorded his homework. Mrs. Sorensen follows through. Brad counts on it.

Frederick

Never has there been a sadder little face than Brad's classmate, Freddy. Freddy looked at me and showed fear before I even spoke. His are the eyes of a small, shaggy puppy being scolded. Like Brad, Freddy has moved around a lot in his 11 years, five schools and four families. He has a brother and two sisters, but he has only seen one of them once, and he doesn't recall which. Just prior to starting the school year with Mrs. Sorensen, Rick, his one-time stepfather, a single father, occasional house painter and welder and seemingly a gentle man, gained legal custody of Freddy. During our interview, Freddy recalled what life was like before he came to live with Rick, and was grateful for the change. Life was better then, shortly after Rick "won" Freddy from foster care, as Freddy put it.

Rick obviously was glad to have Freddy with him and Freddy was happy there when we chatted. Rick loves Freddy—always will. As he leaned forward in his chair, brushing aside cereal spilled on the table by his energetic 5-year-old son from breakfast and rubbing his beard, Rick spoke guardedly but lovingly of Freddy: "He is a *good* kid," he said quietly, "he tries." Rick badly wanted to help Freddy do well in school, but didn't know how to help him, admitting he was a poor student himself and had trouble reading. Nor was he good at setting rules and reinforcing them at home. Like Freddy, he tried, he said. Freddy's behavior puzzles Rick, especially why he didn't regularly turn in his schoolwork: "I have no idea . . . I [can't] figure [it] out." When meeting with school representatives, Rick felt uncomfortable and inadequate, a bit resentful, but still, he said, he wanted to be helpful despite how he feels about school, all schools.

Rick has difficulty supporting Freddy and his son. Finances are tight, work intermittent. The house was Rick's mother's before she died, so there is no worry about having a place to live. Nevertheless, Rick struggles and worries about paying his bills. To help pay bills, the upstairs rooms are rented out to a woman and her daughter. Lacking resources, the house is badly in need of repair; inside it is grubby and much lived-in. Despite Rick's financial problems, the boys have lots of toys, which lay on the floors of every room, signs of a completed game or imaginary adventure.

Since the interviews, conducted at a time when Freddy's future appeared brighter, the situation deteriorated. Details are sketchy or unavailable: rumors about Rick losing his temper and hurting Freddy. Earlier Mrs. Sorensen and the special education teacher began to notice subtle changes in Freddy's behavior. Soon, steps were taken and social services was called in to check on the family. For the second time in Freddy's young life, he was pulled from one family and placed in another, this time in Rick's sister's home. I couldn't discover what happened without asking others to compromise confidences. Apparently, Rick's life collapsed. I have seen Freddy once since the move and he appears happy, as happy as Freddy can be, which is not unhappy.

Before moving into Rick's home, Freddy lived with his mother and her boyfriend, a drug addict. His mother didn't bother to have Freddy attend school for over a year. Neglected, his life was hard, uncertain, dangerous, and eventually he was taken from his mother and placed in foster care. Freddy hasn't seen his biological father since he was an infant, and since being taken from his mother he hears from her only occasionally. She makes appointments to visit Freddy, but never shows up as promised. She calls him on Monday, makes promises of taking him to a movie on Friday, then promises a dinner and a movie, then adds shopping to the growing list of promises. By Friday Freddy can barely contain his excitement. Then, she "forgets." Monday comes again. Hers is a legacy of hurt, yet Freddy still badly wants to see her and wants her love. She may be horrible to him, but still, she is Freddy's mother, and he needs her.

Freddy said that he's certain his academic problems came from having missed so much school: "My mom wouldn't let me go to school, so I am not as smart as all the other kids." Sadly, he doesn't believe he will ever catch up to other children, and thinks of himself as dumb. When I observed him in class he often behaved in ways that confirmed for him the accuracy of that judgment: he didn't do work; or did an assignment but didn't bother to turn it in; or he'd get an assignment wrong, and did sloppy work. It pleases him when another child who he thinks is smart makes a mistake; and when he or she does, if Freddy dares (and he only dared if Mrs. Sorensen was occupied elsewhere), he enjoys teasing them, as though hunting for a weakness to exploit, a weakness that gives him strength. Their failure was his success. But in Mrs. Sorensen's room no one teases anyone, and punishment for perpetrators is swift, sure, and public!

When Freddy is teased he completely crumbles. According to Mrs. Sorensen, he thinks of himself as a victim and plays on others' sympathies even as he is unable to recognize that he has overplayed his hand. No one, however, would deny that he is a victim. One day in the school library, for instance, he crawled underneath a computer desk, curled up, and making a great display of his suffering, refused to come out when asked because someone had made an untoward remark about him. Mrs. Sorensen was forced to drag him out from beneath the desk in order to talk with him, which she did once she got him out of the library and away from the class. The next day, Mrs. Sorensen said, he unmercifully teased Maggie, one of the "smart" kids in class who made a mistake in the geography contest. Until Mrs. Sorensen made the link for him, and she made it loudly, Freddy saw no connection between his having crawled under a desk to hide and suffer the day before and the tears that streamed down Maggie's face following his cruel comments. Mrs. Sorensen was angry; Freddy got the point. Still, this behavior is a far cry from how the year started, when Freddy would respond to any disappointment by exploding into an uncontrollable tantrum, banging his head on his desk, throwing things, screaming, and kicking tables and books. When he behaved like this, other children pulled away. With time and experience in Lafayette, this behavior changed as he learned Mrs. Sorensen wouldn't tolerate it, and that she kept her promises; she would help him and so, too, would the school special educator, whom he came to adore.

As time passed, Freddy smiled more. He engaged in fewer behaviors that confirmed his negative self-assessment and undermined him academically. Slowly he began to discover he didn't need to fail. He even began to work with other children in class, and resisted the temptation to smack or poke them or draw on their papers as they tried to complete their work as he had at the beginning of the year. He also became better able to accept the help of other children, and not worry so much that in accepting their help he was openly admitting he was not as smart as other kids.

While Freddy was at Rick's house he never missed school; to miss was simply unthinkable, even though he'd fail to turn in his work. Besides, if he missed he knew Mrs. Sorensen and the school special educator would check on him. But now Freddy is in another school, his sixth in his short life.

REFLECTIONS

Eric Erikson[2] has written about the need children have for "basic trust." This is the foundation upon which emotional health rests. Children need to have confidence that life is predictable, that adults can be counted on. They need to know that they are valued and loved by others. From basic trust, children can reach out and take the risks that eventually lead to competence. Lacking conditions that enable basic trust, personality nevertheless forms and identity builds. Brad trusts no one and nothing, including himself. He hoarded food until locks were placed on the refrigerator not because he was hungry but because he wasn't certain if he would have food the next day. He steals even when he doesn't need the money, which he puts away or gives away. He knows better, he says, but continues to steal and is puzzled by his behavior.

For Freddy, any attention, even if very negative, is better than no attention at all. Being punished is a sign of being cared for. Handling punishment is easy; handling expressions of love and concern is more difficult. Freddy seems to think of himself as unlovable, as being unworthy of love, so he tests it. In school I witnessed Freddy pushing others until they reacted, sometimes by striking him, other times by crying and withdrawing. I cannot help but wonder, perhaps Freddy was testing Rick when Rick lashed out. Children like Freddy do a lot of testing of others.

Adults often lament the rise of gangs. Gangs are condemned outright. Yet young people join them for good reasons. In addition to providing a sense of belonging and sometimes a perverse sense of safety and security, they also are tightly rule-bound. Gangs provide a measure of predictability.

Mrs. Sorensen understood Brad and Freddy in ways they couldn't possibly understand themselves. She sought to assist Brad's parents and Rick by creating a secure and predictable classroom environment and by loving them despite their antisocial behavior. In her classroom, rules were clear, and so were consequences. Punishment was swift and sure. But so was praise for work well done and expressions of genuine affection. Rules and consequences were implemented within a trustworthy environment, one characterized by emotional honesty, respect, and open and consistent caring. By doubting whether basic trust can be developed if it hasn't been formed at a very early age, Erikson poses a terribly troubling question. Can these boys ever become trusting? Thus far, their life experience hasn't given them reason to become trusting and much must change if they are to change. What is certain is that while in Mrs. Sorensen's classroom and within Lafayette School, both boys eventually became more trusting and behaved in ways that encouraged trust in others even if there were relatively few signs of transfer from one setting to another. Surely this is reason for hope, one that teachers must hold to even as they encounter children whose behavior tries them.

CHAPTER 8

Children's Dreams
of the Future

I asked each of the children if they thought about what they might want
to do or be in the future. Five said they didn't think about the future,
although one of the five said she wanted to be a mom. Josiah, from chapter
4, knew he wanted a job, but he hadn't thought about what he might
want to do, only that he needed to make enough money to realize his
main goal, to take care of others: "I would like having a job. Having
money and taking care of my mom and dad and my kids and my wife."
As mentioned before, Josiah lives with his grandmother and stepgrandfather in their small apartment because his parents neglected and abused
him. Most of the other children had specific ideas about the future, including about their vocations. I asked all the children a genie question, "If I
was an all-powerful genie, and could do anything, and offered you one
wish, what would you wish for that would make you most happy? Remember," I said, "whatever you wish for must make you most happy."

VOCATIONAL IMAGININGS

"For where your treasure is, there will your heart be also."
                                                    —Matthew 6:21

Human hopes and dreams for the future perhaps reveal more about who
we are at our core than any other manifestation of self. What we most
long for and our imagined projections of self into the future, tell who we
are, how we are oriented toward the world. Children imagine many ways
of being in and relating to the world and they test them in imagination.
T.V. is a source of dreams: Randall's idea that he could make a lot of
money as a lawyer came from watching reruns of the series *Matlock*.
Advertising is another source. Adults—parents, grandparents, friends—
also influence children's projections of self into the future. Vincente
thought seriously about being a policeman because at one time, prior to
entering the construction industry, his severely injured and much-loved
father had worn a badge. Vincente wanted to be like his dad.

Over time, these images change as the children change and as their circumstances change. Suddenly, in fifth grade, several of the boys began imagining themselves as professional athletes. Studies of adolescents repeatedly show they have unrealistically high job expectations, and nowhere is this more evident than when boys dream of becoming professional athletes. They overestimate their chances many, many times over. Still, they dream. Strangely, each of the boys who have this dream believe firmly and without exception that they need to attend college to play ball. The diminutive and brilliant game show contestant Rolf was stunned by the idea that college wasn't a requirement for the NBA; he was certain that it was: "Before [playing for the Jazz] I'd go to college because you know how you have to go to college to play basketball." "You do?" I asked. But "Kobe Bryant didn't. Shawn Kemp didn't." "You mean Shawn Kemp didn't go to college to get a basketball degree, for real?!" Rolf asked incredulously. "You don't." "Then how do you play it?" "You just have to be good," I responded. "You also have to be hired?" "Uh-uh." "Rats, that is the one problem." Juan, whose uncle was murdered, could see himself as a Denver Bronco playing in front of huge adoring crowds of fans. Alfredo fantasized shooting jumpers while playing in the NBA; undoubtedly the smallest player in league history, but wealthy, admired, respected. Each genuinely believes their dreams of wealth and fame are realistic, not fanciful at all. Younger boys didn't report such dreams. No girls mentioned athletics.

Second-, third-, and fourth-grade girls imagined themselves teaching. So did two of the third-grade boys. Three boys saw themselves as policemen. Little Dan and a third-grade boy want to be firemen. The book *Clifford the Fire Dog* stirs Little Dan's imagination. Behind the imaginings are values, themes that play the heartstrings of each child, that pluck the song of self: service, justice, artistic expression, and adventure, in addition to the future NBA and NFL hall-of-famers' dreams of wealth and fame gained while playing a game.

As I spoke with the children, I was a bit surprised and touched by how many think of fulfillment coming through service to others. Almost all of the children are deeply concerned about the welfare of others, especially children younger than themselves, including siblings like Alfredo's little tagalong handicapped brother. Given the strong and positive influence of their teachers, it is not surprising that teaching holds a place in so many of the children's dreams for the future. Some of the children appear called to teach, drawn to teaching as the most authentic expression of self. Many teachers feel called. Ten-year-old Arcelia, whose life with her parents was so horrendous and who expressed appreciation for the discipline provided by her teachers, spoke forcefully, confidently about teaching: "I am going to be a teacher." No doubt in her mind. "I like kids . . . I like teaching kids." Teaching so fascinated her that prior to attending Lafayette she actually sought and was given opportunities to teach her classmates: "At my other school . . . they would let me teach the class. . . . I would teach math or reading and it was fun." Clinton also plays teacher. "I want to be a teacher. . . . [Teachers] are fun and they are usually nice and they help you learn better. . . . I think it is fun." He plays teacher with friends: "We just read and stuff and we have someone be the teacher. . . . [The teacher] teaches us math problems and she reads stories and stuff." When he plays the student role he gets in trouble: The teacher disciplines us "for fun . . . we talk and she tells us not to. She puts the name on the board. . . . We would usually go to the principal's office, but that is my mom or their mom." He believes as a teacher he will be able to help children "know hard problems, they can fix them, like math problems." Clinton should know, math mystifies him.

One of Clinton's third-grade classmates, a girl, plays teacher and plans on teaching: "I will be a teacher. . . . It is fun. I have a chalkboard at home and me and my sister, I play the teacher and she is the student. . . . We do math class, reading, social studies. . . . I made a little book out of paper and it has [math] problems for my sister to do." Sometimes she finds it necessary to discipline her seventh-grade sister and the sister resists: "I make her stand in the corner." "How do you make her do that?" "Well, I say that if you don't go to the corner I will tell mommy." Again, mother is the principal! This child's goals are clear: she will go to college, where she will "need to pass a lot of tests" to become a teacher. Another of Clinton's classmates, this time a boy, thought teaching "looks fun." "Why?" "Well teaching is fun because helping kids learn; like if we didn't have no school everyone would be retarded. Almost everyone." By teaching, he said he will help others to avoid becoming retarded! A sixth-grade student enrolled in resource wants to be a physician and a singer. "I want to learn and I want to work in a hospital. I like helping people," she said.

A desire for justice for others, and perhaps mercy for oneself, is at the heart of some of the children's future dreams. These children think of themselves as having suffered at the hands of others and they want justice, a world where good guys win and bad guys get their just desserts. They long for a world seemingly quite different from the one they inhabit, where trust is frequently misplaced. One first-grader wants to be a policeman. "Why do you want to be a policeman?" I asked. "Policemen help people a lot. They help get better places." "What will be a better place?" "All the places where all the police are. . . . You can help the town get better, like not have as much bad people." "How do police help do that?"

"Because they catch them, and take them to jail. [Police] can try to catch a whole bunch [of bad guys] and then you just get a better place. There wouldn't be so much violence and break-ins. Someone broke into our house. So, they won't do that and there won't be anymore of the drug things." "Somebody broke into your house?" "Yeah." "What happened?" "They stole some CDs and stuff." He wants justice. But he also wants to make his neighborhood a safer place for others. Marshall, who is so deeply disturbed, also wants to be "a cop." "Why?" "Because nobody can hit me." "Do you know any policemen?" "Mr. Lange [his teacher], he was a policeman." Marshall will use his power to get even with his enemies. Police, he believes, "can smack, punch, kick." His immediate concern is with his sister: "My sister, smacks me in the face. . . . It hurts." An eye for an eye, a tooth for a tooth is Marshall's conception of justice. He'll fix her; justice will be served with a punch, a kick. I was amazed that no child, not one, mentioned punishment of an adult for neglect or for abuse. Getting even is more of a horizontal than a vertical affair: peers, not parents, get punished.

A few children find pleasure in thinking about artistic creation as having a central place in their futures. Big Bad Zeke nearly exploded with enthusiasm as he imagined himself being an architect and designing buildings: "I could . . . be an architect because I have all of these funky buildings in my head. . . . I can draw funky buildings. . . . They just come into my head. I can draw one, it is something for scientists, like [a] Frankenstein building. It is like a scientist lab but it doesn't make people come alive. I could draw one for you." He began drawing, and I had to agree, it was funky, all right. Zeke also contemplates doing cartoon voices. Forrest Gump, I learned, is his specialty: "'Mama always said, life is like a box of chocolates. You never know what you are going to get.'" One of Zeke's classmates, a girl, dreams of being an artist. If she doesn't get into the army (but she thinks she will because she is "very tough"), Jeri would like to be a singer.

Seeking high adventure, Rolf and Sally both want to be astronauts, although the NBA would be all right with Rolf in a pinch. Rolf is having second thoughts about going into space, however: "I have always wanted to be an astronaut, but since I have known that some things may go wrong that you may not be able to fix, [I'm not certain] . . . I could be part of mission control." "Mostly," Sally said, she dreams of being "an astronaut, that's my true dream. I really try to study hard just to be one." If she can't fly into space, she'd love to be a musician.

Relationship, power, and money are the dominant themes that ran through the children's responses to the genie question. As already mentioned, many children wanted to be with their fathers, including boys whose fathers are dead. Others wanted a dad. Josiah longed for his sister and his grandmother: "I had my Grandma Tina, she died, and sometimes I wish she came back." She was good to him, gentle, loving. "To bring my uncle and my great-grandma back and to just give us a house with a whole bunch of animals," was Juan's greatest wish. Shane wants his parents reunited. One of the third-grade girls wants to change her sister so they'll get along better: "Most of the time she's always being mean to me . . . but when I am angry and when she says, 'I'm sorry', she says, 'will you forgive me?' I say, 'No.'" "Why do you say no?" "Because sometimes she really makes me mad and I can't forgive her." Mark desperately fears that someday he will be returned to his father and wishes for another father: "I would like it if [my uncle] was my father. . . . That would be *the* best." Freddy remarked: "I would bring back my grandpa and grandma. . . . I lived with my grandpa for about a year." He died. Freddy also thought it would be marvelous if he could permanently sever a few relationships: "When everybody I hate is on earth and everybody I like is in heaven and I'm dead, too." "That will make you happy?" "Uh-huh. I will be with everybody, even God." "Are there really people you hate?" "Uh-huh." "Like who?" "Let's see. I hate Juan, because he always pushes me. He hits me in the ribs and then he falls down, not me." Juan sets Freddy up for teacher punishment, or so Freddy thinks. Freddy also found Sally and Chuck more than a little irritating and he'd be pleased if he never sees them again. He got this wish.

If one of the first-grade boys had the help of an all-powerful genie he'd "help the entire earth. . . . Like help the poor get money to have houses and get all of them happy. Have the entire earth be a better place. . . . Like help everybody that was having hard times." This boy's family knows hard times, yet his thoughts are on others. "Do you know anybody having a hard time?" I asked. "Yeah." "Who?" "My sister's husband is having a really hard time. He had something in his tummy that was growing. He had an operation." A second-grader knows exactly what he would do with great power: "Stop people from taking drugs. . . . I just don't like it. [And I don't like it] when people smoke cigarettes and I am around, like in the car, I don't like it because it gets in my face." "What would make you really happy?" I asked Chuck. "Peace. . . . Because the more wars there are, the more people die." With the help of her genie, Jeri would "protect animals from poachers." If Tanner was all-powerful, he would "Make all of the dogs that die, not die, live and have food." Tanner loves his dog, Salty, who comforts and delights him: I can only be grateful Tanner's power is limited, that I'm the genie and I can say "No." Katherine's greatest desire is: "The people who like steal and stuff, to make them good and not do bad things."

A third-grade student wants to be "rich," but not for herself. "I want a swing set and a puppy and a lot more stuff. I would get [my family] a big house. It would be two-story. I'll have all kinds of art on the walls. It will have swing sets and I'll have a pool." A second-grader has the same dream: "To get a house . . . blue . . . it is light blue and dark blue with tiles on the roof . . . a blue door . . . the whole house is light blue except for the checkered tiles and the door. . . . It would be big. A garden [with] vegetables and some grapevines. . . . A cherry tree or an apple tree . . . window benches, window seats." She has thought carefully about this, no more apartment living. Rolf also dreams of a house, but one near the school. Zeke simply likes the idea of being wealthy: "Three hundred tons of gold . . . that would make me more than happy. That would make me excited." Charity shares Zeke's unbridled enthusiasm for images of excessive consumption, lifestyles of the rich and famous. J. B. would like to be "rich" as well so she can buy a new bike. "I want a new bike because my dad tried to go to his work and fix my bike because my sister was on it, and she was twelve, and she was sitting on it, and she made it flat so my dad tried to go to his work and fix it. Then he tried to get someone to fix it and he couldn't fix it." J. B. believes one needs to be wealthy to buy a new bike. Perhaps she is right.

REFLECTIONS

Hope does not demand a belief in progress. It demands a belief in justice: a conviction that the wicked will suffer, that wrongs will be made right, that the underlying order of things is not flouted with impunity. Hope implies a deep-seated trust in life that appears absurd to those who lack it. It rests on confidence not so much in the future as in the past. It derives from early memories—no doubt distorted, overlaid with later memories, and thus not wholly reliable as a guide to any factual reconstruction of past events. . . . Such experience leaves as its residue the unshakable conviction, not that the past was better than the present, but that trust is never completely misplaced either.[1]

Hopefulness is among the factors that enable children to survive and to eventually recover from severe adversity. Other factors will be discussed in the next, and concluding, chapter. The hold of hope on some of the children is tenuous. Present events and the memories they build layer on past memories to suggest wrongs will not be righted, that whatever order there is to the world is capricious, untrustworthy, and fundamentally unfair. Tenacious, Sally hasn't yet given up, but her grip on hope is slipping, weakened by continuous blows to her spunky spirit: yet another new father, another new school, another meal to cook for others to eat and no one to help clean up.

At least eight of the children live strictly in the present. No yesterday. No tomorrow. For these children, excluding Mark, low or no expectations prevent disappointment. Based on their long experience with the adults in their lives—but not the teachers at Lafayette—the boundaries of normal behavior are broad and expanding. Few standards are stable enough to tie one's sense of self to. It is not wise to seriously contemplate the future. The path of least resistance may become irresistible. The teachers of these children face no greater challenge than to help them imagine themselves differently, not as they think they are, but as potentially capable people who have talent awaiting development, who can achieve, and who deserve good things. Proof of potential requires more than mere words, words like those spoken by Sally's mother, words of warning, desperate but hollow. Mark could not accept that he deserved a good Christmas. Freddy had trouble believing he could ever earn a decent grade, and was unconvinced that hard work pays off.

It is easy to dismiss problems of this kind as reflections of low self-esteem. Unfortunately, in the current social context, building self-esteem is usually thought of as a matter of helping children and adults feel good about themselves without recognizing that competence is the only solid foundation for self-respect and competence involves meeting established standards. Juan seems to have learned this lesson on the football field but not in the classroom. Rolf learned it playing a mud puddle in the first-grade school play and from sharing in conversation his remarkable, effulgent intellectual abilities and noticing how others reacted with interest and delight. As Rolf knows, reading makes one interesting. Growing competence and the confidence that flows from increasingly successful performance are crucial to forming a healthy identity, for self-love, and for sustaining hope in troubled times.

There is another side to self-esteem, an especially dark side, that requires brief mention here. Studies of young gang members reveal they often have high self-esteem, grounded in group membership. Membership makes them unteachable. Moreover, self-esteem can be raised by lowering children's expectations for themselves. By lowering expectations children can be made to feel good about poor or mediocre performance, and costs can be deferred to the future. In short, teachers who are seduced into thinking most behavior problems and student failure come from low self-esteem need to do some rethinking. Especially they must resist the temptation to reinforce children's patterns of maladaptation by confirming unhealthy and distorted conceptions of self.[2]

Competence requires seeing connections between current behaviors and future outcomes. Such connections elude many of the children. The one connection most make is that good grades are required for good jobs.

This is an argument, a mantra, made by some parents and by many teachers, even elementary teachers, and it's one that cannot be sustained fully as many of the children will learn later in high school. There simply are not enough good jobs to go around. Disillusionment follows when the children eventually discover the truth. As Rolf said, he thought anyone could play in the NBA if they went to college and received a "basketball degree." The idea that players are hired never occurred to him, and the thought was deflating. Mark couldn't accept the idea. Nor could Chuck. Many of the children have heard adults speak about the importance of attending college, although they have little concept of what that means— more school like elementary school is their best guess.

This said, it is wonderful that so many of these children, whose lives are so very complex and at times harsh, find pleasure in one or another of their studies. Accomplishment in one area may positively influence accomplishment in other areas, but most importantly it influences how the children think about themselves and the future. For those children doing well in school, suggestions that good grades are important for future jobs is less important than the present pleasures found in their studies: Katherine's love of reading and fascination with the meaning of words. Rolf's exuberance for astronomy. Brad's enjoyment of mathematics. A classmate's pleasure in art. Despite being "in the middle," as he said, Freddy likes mathematics, but he hates reading (except *The Boxcar Children*). A third-grader was thrilled to report that she'd just received yet another 100 on her "times tests." She studied, succeeded, and it felt very, very good and she wanted to share her triumph with me. Arguing that good grades are essential for future work is to play to a child's fears, and these children have too many other concerns to allow this one to climb to the top of the list.

Fear of failure does not motivate these children to strive for success. Many know failure, and it isn't as bad as it's cracked up to be. Just ask them. Not trying means not failing, and not failing helps protect an already fragile self. Those who do well do so primarily because they like what they do well—success feels good—and especially because good performance is important to others they care deeply about including dedicated mothers, grandparents and, of course, teachers. The children all said their teachers want them to do well. The children I interviewed easily recognized this quality in their teachers, signs of dedication, none of indifference—Lafayette teachers care. Proof of caring is not found only in a willingness to reward but also in some surprising forms, like Arcelia's desire for discipline and Chuck's expectation of punishment. Teachers who do not discipline children, who do not punish inappropriate behavior, do not care. The children believe this, and they are right. Doing well and meeting a recognized standard strengthens a child's resolve and brings a handful of hope.

The children's concern for others, animals, and the earth amazes and inspires and speaks to their goodness. So often children characterized as "at-risk" are portrayed in various media as damaged goods, as threats to civility and decency, as lacking redeeming qualities. These children's dreams suggest otherwise. Perhaps such characterizations are accurate for some children—although I am not certain of this—but not for those with whom I spoke. Some of their parents are infuriating, but the children are not. Not these children. All are hurting, some are desperate, but nearly all long for a better world, to be a good friend, a good student, to make their parents—even as disconnected and lost as some of their parents are—proud. They want to make a positive contribution in the lives of others. Some want to take care of their parents since they seem unable to care for themselves. Chuck, who lives in fear, wants peace. The sometimes homeless Randall, a boy who lacks even a bed and is often knocked around by his older brother, worries about global warming, that the "world is going to overheat," and wonders what can be done about it. Sally had one wish: "*My* one wish," she said, "is for people to just be kind to each other. That's it."

CHAPTER 9

For the Sake of Children

CHILDREN'S CHANGES

I asked each child a variation of the first genie question: "I'm the genie again: What would you have me change in Lafayette that would make you happier, or make the school a better place for you?"

Universally, the children said they enjoy school and feel cared for, and that they respect their teachers and feel respected by them. Most love Lafayette. Nevertheless, they had some serious and not-so-serious recommendations to make that would improve Lafayette, they thought, beginning with school lunch, a serious recommendation. Eating is a concern to many of the children, so we ought to take their suggestions seriously. "To have lunch for half an hour and you could get more food," a second grader said. She would like it if her genie made it so she could get seconds. A third-grade student wants to have lunch sooner: "Because sometimes I get really hungry during class." She'd also like a second helping. One of her classmates agrees, classes ought "to go to lunch faster." He gets hungry, too. Chuck wants greater variety in the food served. The day I spoke with Little Dan there had been a fight, and he was worried. The school, he thought, would be improved if there wasn't any fighting: "There is a lot of fighting going on today. Kenny, somebody kicked him right here in the head." Little Dan touched his head, showing where Kenny was hurt, and looked very concerned. Brad "would kick out all of the bullies." Feeling a bit of the martyr, Sally agrees: Get rid of "the *bullies*. There's a ton of them here. They pick on me after school." A first-grader thought it would be terrific if there were "more teachers, so there would be more to help our schoolmates." A girl, a third-grader, agreed. A boy in the second grade wanted more slides on the playground. "The soccer field could be made out of grass instead of concrete," Tanner said. He likes playing soccer and asphalt gets hot and prevents good play. Juan, the kid with attitude, was bothered that the kindergartners had so little playground space: "The playground, make it a lot bigger for the little kindergartners. Like half of it, so . . . they could have their own half." Some children thought longer recesses would be wonderful. So, more food, more teachers, fewer troublemakers, longer recesses, and Lafayette would be a better school. Not a bad list. Remarkably, a few of the children are aware that more teachers are needed, that their teachers are working extremely hard, perhaps too hard. Two or 3 hours after school is dismissed one usually sees lights on in classrooms where teachers are busily preparing for the next day's lessons or grading papers. Mostly, the children think Lafayette is just fine the way it is. The majority of the children offered no recommendations whatsoever for improving Lafayette. Without exception, they are convinced their teachers want them to learn, care about them, and are good at what they do. As Mapa said about Mrs. Novakovich: "She is fun. . . . She knows me, I know her, she is a great teacher." Randall thinks Mr. DeCourse "is funny. He helps you with your assignments. He lets you have extra time on them, on your reports and stuff. He lets you go on the computers and look up things. He likes to read *Phantom of the Opera*." This is high praise from Randall, who has never before been a fan of schooling or of teachers. He's similarly full of praise for the special education teacher: She's "full of energy. She plays sports with us. She plays football with us and basketball. She's pretty good at it, too. She can catch, she can throw." This teacher has proven herself on the playing field! The children feel safe, love the library, all have favorite subjects and say they are trying to do well, even those who are not performing adequately, like Clinton, the boy with the long, wavy hair who wants to be a teacher. The children are happy at Lafayette, and perhaps there is no better measure of whether or not a school is succeeding than this. As one girl said when I asked her if she would avoid coming to school if she could: "No. Cuz I want to learn." I believe she speaks for nearly all the children.

Having spent many hours inside Lafayette, I believe I understand the children's feelings. I also like being there. It's a comfortable place. Clean. Lively. Friendly. Safe. There is a feeling of unforced orderliness. It's also a place that is purposeful, a place where children and adults are joined together in a common cause.

THE SCHOOL CONTEXT

The teachers and principal at Lafayette have succeeded in creating a positive learning climate in the school. Children expect to learn and expect to be cared for by their teachers. Teachers know nearly all the students in the school by name. No child is invisible. I don't believe any child slips through the cracks; they are missed when missing. As earlier mentioned, there are two programs in the building, a neighborhood program with about 325 children and a gifted and talented program that enrolls just over 200. In the past there has been serious tension between the children and the parents of the two programs. For a time some of the neighborhood children felt bullied by the children in the gifted and talented program who staked out portions of the playground as their own and in other ways let the neighborhood children know of their inferior status. But over the last several years a concerted effort encouraged by the current and previous principal has been made to break down barriers and promote positive interaction between the two groups through team-teaching and shared projects and celebrations. Relationships are better now.

Mostly, the tensions have been and are grounded in social class differences, not race, not ethnicity, not language. A few children still show a little resentment for what they see as the privileged status of the children in the gifted and talented program. Overall, the presence of the gifted and talented program has been a mixed blessing. Some academically able children have been skimmed from the neighborhood program and with them go their parents, a rich and wonderful resource for teachers and other students that is missed and badly needed. This said, many parents prefer to have their children in the neighborhood program because of the much greater diversity of the student population and because of the recognized quality of the teachers who are well-known and highly re-garded. Despite student and parent skimming and occasional expressions of tension, the children in the gifted and talented program and their teachers, who the past 3 years have worked closely with their colleagues teaching in the neighborhood program, make a significant and positive contribution to maintaining and sustaining the entire school's academic focus. Such a focus is key to school success.

Classes are large. It is not unusual to find a class of 30 or more students—far too many. Over the past 3 decades a good deal of research has been conducted on the effects of class size on student learning. Most often learning has been measured by standardized achievement tests that generally favor direct instruction—a teacher standing in front of the class talking and *directing* students—over other more active and interactive instructional models. Not surprisingly, given this measure, the advantage of small over large classes has not been judged significant. The debate has been misguided, however. The reason small class size is important for students and their teachers has less to do with student academic performance than with relationship building and encouraging positive student behavior, behavior that enhances learning and feelings of connect-edness to the school and to other children. Large classes inhibit the devel-opment of caring but honest relationships between children and teachers and among children. Given the large size of classes, there simply are too many children for teachers to discuss each frequently and thoughtfully.

In responding to changing demographics, teaching within Lafayette appears to have changed in some ways over the years. The challenge has been to keep student learning, not control, as the central aim. Orderliness is a precondition for learning, and many urban school faculties struggle mightily to gain and to maintain it. Sometimes order becomes its own end. Keeping focused on learning is not easy, particularly as increasing numbers of schoolchildren attend who are prone to act out and who require consistent adult attention and guidance. What has not changed is that the teachers remain "people who are intrinsically moved to be lifelong learners and who need no extrinsic reward to learn more about music, botany, philately, computer technology, or fish breeding. Children of poverty rarely, if ever, see such people, even on television." This is one of the essential characteristics of the "star teachers" identified by Martin Haberman in his study of teachers who are effective with urban children and youth.[1] And it is a characteristic common to the teachers I observed and interviewed. These teachers are dedicated to learning and to improving their practice.

There are some indications that a "pedagogy of poverty" is giving way to "good teaching" within the school.[2] A pedagogy of poverty, in contrast to good teaching, is composed of giving information, asking questions, giving directions, making assignments, monitoring seatwork, reviewing assignments, giving tests, reviewing tests, assigning homework, reviewing homework, settling disputes, punishing noncompliance, marking papers, and giving grades. These actions are what most adults recall as the essence of teaching, that are embedded in the "grammar of schooling," the taken-for-granted ways that schools conduct business.[3] Such practices fail to motivate and educate children at risk and may even add to their troubles. Moreover, they fail to maintain teacher interest and commitment.

Drawing on a growing body of research on teaching practices that have positive results for the learning of urban children and youth, Martin Haberman of the University of Wisconsin-Milwaukee argues that a pedagogy of poverty needs to be replaced with another, and conflicting, pedagogy. He suggests the following principles need to be embraced:

1. Whenever students are involved with issues they regard as vital concerns, good teaching is going on.
2. Whenever students are involved with explanations of human differences, good teaching is going on.

3. Whenever students are being helped to see major concepts, big ideas, and general principles and are not merely engaged in the pursuit of isolated facts, good teaching is going on.
4. Whenever students are involved in planning what they will be doing, it is likely that good teaching is going on.
5. Whenever students are involved with applying ideals such as fairness, equity, or justice to their world, it is likely that good teaching is going on.
6. Whenever students are actively involved, it is likely that good teaching is going on.
7. Whenever students are directly involved in a real-life experience, it is likely that good teaching is going on.
8. Whenever students are actively involved in heterogenous groups, it is likely that good teaching is going on.
9. Whenever students are asked to think about an idea in a way that questions common sense or a widely accepted assumption, which relates new ideas to ones learned previously, or which applies an idea to the problems of living, then there is a chance that good teaching is going on.
10. Whenever students are involved in redoing, polishing, or perfecting their work, it is likely that good teaching is going on.
11. Whenever teachers involve students with the technology of information access, good teaching is going on.
12. Whenever students are involved in reflecting on their own lives and how they have come to believe and feel as they do, good teaching is going on.

In short, teachers who embrace these principles teach for meaning.[4] This is not to say that children are never drilled in math facts, but it is to say that drill plays a supporting role in the larger goal of achieving meaning. Adults who are interested in helping children may need to get used to a different kind of schooling than they are familiar with, and this may produce a bit of discomfort and perhaps criticism.

Evidence of these principles was abundant in my observations within Lafayette classrooms. Not all classrooms fit this pattern, but much of what went on in them did fit. Surely this is one reason why the children like school so much and feel valued by their teachers, even when they had difficulties in previous schools. Remarkably, I do not believe the teachers were taught these principles; rather, I believe they discovered many of them as they sought to be more effective in their classrooms with a changing population of students. The sharp focus on children's learning led them in this direction.

The teachers work very hard in Lafayette. As the year wears on, signs of exhaustion begin to show. With the rapidly changing student population, where more and more children need more and more help, and where greater numbers of children live distressing lives, I wonder when the teachers' energy will run out and the learning climate will deteriorate. With no increase in resources for the school or any reduction in teaching load, and continued politically inspired attacks on teacher character and ability, I fear eventually something will give. As it is, policy makers support pathology over prevention. In the meantime, Lafayette teachers continue to seek better ways of touching the lives of children, sometimes having to conduct a kind of educational triage; the most serious "cases" get attended to first.

CHANGING THE WORKPLACE

A few changes in the workplace specific to Lafayette, but likely connected to schools across this country, would greatly assist the teachers to better achieve their educational aims. Those who care about children and their future can help bring about these changes, some of which are probably obvious. Already I've mentioned that Lafayette classes are very large. Dramatically lowering class size would have immense benefits for the children and for teachers, although there is a point of diminishing returns. Even a small reduction would help. Over the past few decades there has been a huge increase in the number of noninstructional personnel in American schools. Ironically, much of the increase has resulted from changing student demographics and the creation of special programs. A compelling case has been made by the National Commission on Teaching and America's Future[5] for returning many of the resources spent on support personnel to the classroom. This would also likely enable improvement in teacher salaries. At Lafayette, for instance, by district policy there is a floating teacher of the gifted and talented who does occasional lessons in neighborhood program classrooms. It's an odd use of a teacher position, one that offers little if any benefit to children or teachers. Returning this one person to full-time teaching would slightly lower class size. How school resources are allocated is a question that ought to be raised by citizens, teachers, and administrators, and pursued at every grade level in every school in America. Resources must be returned to the classroom. As good as the relationships are between Lafayette teachers and children, they could be better merely by reducing student numbers even slightly.

Given the changes in demographics at Lafayette, there are fewer and fewer parents who are able and willing to volunteer in their children's

classrooms. Schools that have extremely high minority populations and
poverty rates qualify for federal funding for hiring aides and other adults
to assist teachers. Many of these classrooms have one or two extra adults
to help the children. As noted, Lafayette, even with a poverty rate standing
at about 45 percent and rising, doesn't qualify for additional funding. But
as we have seen, poverty rates tell only part of the children's story; poverty
isn't the only condition that puts children at-risk. A modest investment
of additional funds in schools like Lafayette, schools where the number
of children with severe emotional, psychological, intellectual, and social
challenges is increasing and where teachers are just holding their own,
would yield dramatic dividends. The federal government could and
should step into this void, in part because a significant portion of the
demographic shift in schools like Lafayette is a direct result of federal
immigration and housing policies. This said, the Lafayette teachers' main
concern is not to have parents come into the classroom, although they
are grateful when they do, but rather to encourage parents to spend time
with their children on schoolwork so the children feel supported at home
and learning is valued.

There are a variety of strategies available for increasing the number
of stable and morally centered adults in classrooms. There are good reasons for doing so. The most effective means for preventing early reading
failure, which is crucial to school success and to building legitimate and
productive self-esteem, are those that incorporate tutoring. While being
tutored by a certified teacher produces the greatest positive results, "the
reading outcomes for all forms of tutoring are very positive. . . . "[6] With
minimal training, older children and youth can be very effective tutors.
Lafayette has been adopted by a large health care organization that brings
a few adults into the school and provides much-needed help, including
procuring computers. This is one program that is making a positive difference. A university program places a few volunteers in the school as part
of a growing emphasis on service learning. In addition, a local church
recently has become a partner with Lafayette. The intention of this program is to provide a pool of adult volunteers that teachers can tap for
tutors, and also for room mothers, aides, and the like. Senior citizens will
make up much of this pool. A thoughtful and sincere invitation extended
by a school faculty to a local religious congregation to become involved
in the education of children is one that is likely to be honored. Lafayette
teachers hunger for the help and actively seek volunteers who are warmly
welcomed into the school.

The aim of bringing more resources into Lafayette is to provide the
teachers with support needed to do what they already do and know how
to do well, not change it in any fundamental way. So much of the current

debate about American schooling centers on words like "restructuring" and "reforming." The assumption is that something is fundamentally wrong with American education, and especially with teachers. Despite frequent and politically motivated attacks on teachers and public schooling, the evidence is simply overwhelming—there are a great many more effective than ineffective schools, and American citizens know it.[7] Political palaver condemns the system outright, and encourages parents who can to flee with their children. I'm increasingly convinced the key to improving schooling is to better play to strengths than to worry over weaknesses. Lafayette teachers clearly know how to provide high-quality education for the children; they only need means adequate to do it and the means are relatively modest.

FOCUSING ON PEOPLE

Improving schools is first and foremost a people problem. Unfortunately, less than 1 percent of the money spent on public education in America goes toward teacher professional development. Having quality teachers in every child's classroom is perhaps the most powerful educational means for improving student performance. For instance, "A Texas study of 900 districts found that teacher expertise explained 40 percent of the difference in student achievement and most of the performance gap between African-American and white students."[8] Clearly, teacher development is school reform.

Rewarding teachers to improve the quality of their teaching will help improve schools, especially since American teachers are consistently underpaid in comparison with their similarly educated peers.[9] Yet instead of focusing on rewards, increasingly attention is being given to forms of punishment which are working their way into educational policy and law. Punishment is unlikely to motivate teachers to substantially increase their skill levels. New York, California, South Carolina, and Texas are among the almost two dozen states that either have adopted plans or have plans in place for rating schools based on student achievement test scores.[10] Some of these states have systems in place for punishing poorly performing schools while others, including Kentucky, Maryland, and North Carolina, also have systems for rewarding those that score well. In Delaware, recent legislation links teacher job reviews to student performance on standardized tests. Even as this law was passed, concern was expressed: "One of the considerations . . . is making sure that teachers who take the toughest jobs, such as those in high-poverty low-performing schools, aren't driven out or discouraged."[11]

Conditions need to be created within schools that support teacher development. Minimally, time within the workday should be set aside for teacher education, including time to study one's own practice. Abundant opportunities to interact and problem-solve with other teachers and parents are needed. Provision for ongoing and informed feedback on teaching and for discussion of the results of teacher evaluation is required. And teachers need access to promising practices and the educational resources to support experimenting with those practices. All citizens have an interest in assuring that these conditions are created within the nation's schools.

Urban schools with large poor, immigrant, and minority student populations consistently perform less well than do their suburban counterparts. In "schools with poverty rates of 25 percent or higher, both poor and better-off youngsters do less well academically. Growing evidence also suggests those schools get less funding than schools in more affluent communities."[12] In the meantime, having acceptable test scores, suburban school leaders can ignore the educational and life challenges of poorly performing children. Despite the reforms of the 1980s that produced a brief narrowing of achievement gaps, the gap between white, Asian, Hispanic, Native American, and black children persists. Continuing to beat up and blame teachers for the persistence of this gap and of school failure will only encourage the most able teachers to leave teaching and demoralize those who remain. No one wins.

ALTERING THE GRAMMAR OF SCHOOLING
AND BOLSTERING RESILIENCY

Skilled teachers are among the most precious of all educational resources. But for the sake of children like those in Mrs. Sorensen's class, Bradley, Sally, Juan, Chuck, Freddy, and Mark, and for the sake of teachers, the grammar of schooling needs changing. The watchwords of schooling, as I've written elsewhere,[13] ought to be: small and simple is better than large and complex. Personal is always and everywhere better than impersonal. Depth is more important than breadth, depth in the study of academic content and in human relationships. Lafayette teachers take the first two of these principles seriously, and to a degree also the third. Sadly, as Mr. DeCourse the sixth-grade teacher observed, once the children leave Lafayette and enter junior high school, what they encounter is an affront to each principle: too many teachers, too many classes, too many students, much curricular fragmentation and too little inquiry. Perhaps there is no better argument than this one for K–12 schools, like those in California that are proving to be successful with inner-city children, or for "looping," keeping children and teachers together for a few years. Mr. DeCourse feared that the good that Lafayette achieved with some of its students like Alfredo will quickly be washed out by the stress of trying to cope with the large scale and factorylike conditions of junior high school, the most irrational of all educational administrative creations. Mr. DeCourse is probably right, but only in part because of the difficulty of adjusting to life in junior high school. Alfredo lacks some of the personal qualities and many of the relationships and forms of support that encourage individual resilience. Depth and consistency of relationship is extremely important.

Across the country, east to west, north to south, one hears the slogan, "All children can learn." It's said solemnly, as though the phrase carries a profound moral weightiness and truth. It's certainly true: some children seem to do well in school when the smart money says they will fail. There is a small but growing research literature on individual resilience that speaks to the experience of most of the children I interviewed.[14] Some children possess qualities that help them handle adversity more effectively than other children; these children lend credence to the slogan. Having special talents or abilities—like Juan's skills on the football field—produces feelings of accomplishment and opens imagination to future possibilities. Religious faith helps sustain children through difficulty by providing perspective on adversity and giving purpose to it. Good intellectual skills, especially including the ability to read well, are important assets, ones that teachers understand and seek to build. Liking oneself and self-confidence have a buffering effect. And having an adult who genuinely believes in and supports a child's sense of self as a worthwhile person is crucially important. In the best of all worlds, children have parents who make them feel worthwhile and valued and whose behavior is predictable, consistent. Lacking parents who behave in these ways, other adults must step forward, people who teach these same lessons consistently and who strengthen children's ability to bounce back from adversity. Such people build hope—faith in the future grounded in the experience of the past.

Children desperately need mentors, adults who model appropriate behavior, coach it, and reinforce such behavior in others, and schools are one place where they should meet. Mentors are more than friends. "Research has shown that if children and youth can form a meaningful and caring bond or attachment with at least one family member or significant adult, their chances of a successful, healthy outcome are very high, even in those families that are facing severe challenges, such as poverty, chemical dependency, and abuse or violence."[15] Mentors assist children as they confront troubling times and help them think problems through in ways that increase their problem-solving ability and competence. They provide new opportunities for children and support them as they confront new challenges. And they protect them from danger.

Creating an educational context that allows teachers and other adults to respond more fully, empathetically, intelligently, and sensitively to children in need is a first-order priority, one that dramatically influences how or even whether a child will achieve academically. To do this requires changing the grammar of schooling.

THE WIDER CONTEXT

Over the course of the past century Americans came to think of virtually all social problems as problems for the schools to solve, including the spread of AIDS, bad driving, drug usage, incivility, and racism. The list is long, the problems numerous and persistent. No wonder disappointment followed. The larger issue of educational reform is often ignored: *What resources and social conditions need to be in place outside of the schools to assure all children optimal opportunities to learn within school?* To say all children can learn without creating conditions supportive of learning is simply bad faith.

For several of the children I interviewed, prenatal care coupled with drug treatment for addicted mothers may have dramatically increased the likelihood of future school and life success. Too late to help Marshall's health, his mother changed her life. Little Dan's mother drank herself to death and left behind a child who will face a lifelong struggle to concentrate and to learn. Josiah's mother gave her children away. Universal health care for children and expectant mothers is desperately needed, as is a system of federally sponsored and certified residential drug treatment facilities for mothers and their children. Consider: hospital charges, physician fees and maternity costs for a birth complicated by substance abuse are about eight times what a normal birth costs—$50,000 compared to $6,300—and this is just the beginning. Much greater emphasis must be placed on educating mothers.

An aggressive national program to provide affordable housing for all families is required, one based on the value of mixing income levels, social classes, and stabilizing neighborhoods. The foolishness of concentrating public housing and shelters in one location is now well understood, but the political will needed to do what is right for the children of poverty is often lacking. As I write, the battered woman's shelter near Lafayette is being greatly enlarged. When children must move, means are required so they can stay in the same school: a bus pass, a roving shuttle if need be.

Stress must be reduced: stress at home, in the neighborhood, as well as within school. Nothing is more important to children than to be surrounded by stable and loving adults, the more the better; but a few will do. Frequent partner-changing, ugly divorce proceedings, unsafe neighborhoods, crime, hunger, and even bullying on the school playground undermine hope. To live only in the here and now as a means for coping with uncertainty and for avoiding disappointment invites disaster for children and for society. Indifference to tomorrow insures moral itinerancy today. Actively discouraging teenage pregnancy and encouraging birth control are important preventative measures. How best to do this is another matter, one requiring serious and ongoing policy discussions involving leaders in social service, health care, government, religion, and education. In such discussions ideological purity is of less importance than performance, strategies that produce results. Moving toward mediation and counseling in divorce proceedings is a positive development for children as well as parents. When marriage produces children, children's rights and well-being must be the central consideration in any legal determination, more important than parental rights and well-being.

Poverty stresses children. Schools can and do feed children, millions of them, often their best meals of the day. To avoid embarrassing a child who receives free or reduced lunch, it must be kept secret. Health centers can and ought to be linked to if not placed within schools and made available to all children. Poor children typically receive poor quality health care. A program is now in place at Lafayette that connects children and their families to various social service agencies. Also, there is a teacher-supported program that provides warm clothing to children in need when winter arrives. When children are ill at ease, they experience stress. As an aside, it is amazing how much medication teachers are required to dispense to children daily. While these medications may help student performance, I doubt the wisdom of this common practice. I know teachers would be glad to pass this responsibility to others, along with the need to conduct periodic lice checks! The jury is still out on congressional welfare reform; initial results are mixed. In Wisconsin, for example, after 2 years 62 percent of recipients found their way into the economy in some fashion, but 38 percent have not. Sixty-two percent may or may not be an impressive accomplishment. Although more expensive than programs that simply seek to reduce the welfare roles, programs like that in Minnesota which allows families to keep receiving benefits until their incomes are 40 percent above the poverty level appear to help stabilize families and encourage development of work-related skills.[16] But the question that policy makers must ask is how the lives of children are being affected. The quality of the children's lives is the measure that matters.

A CONCLUDING THOUGHT

Americans have gotten used to crisis metaphors that no longer stir us, especially not in good times when the Dow averages fixate attention and incite imagination. We are weary of Washington, increasingly distrustful of the free press, and many of us are self-absorbed and experiencing an ideological hardening of the arteries. Historically a generous people—and most Americans are generous still—we've become quite cynical about government and distrustful of others unlike ourselves, especially those we see as dependent. When we look around us, it is surely true, there is an incredible number of numbskulls running around claiming all the rights without accepting any of the responsibilities of citizenship or of parenting, but they are rich and poor alike. Hundreds of thousands of children—probably millions—have been born to lousy parents: drugged, lazy, uneducated, bitter, indifferent, dishonest, disengaged, selfish. Pick the descriptor, and then consider whether or not a measure of pleasure is felt once the label is placed, and the finger pointing done. Placing blame has become an American passion and pastime. Somehow many of us believe something or someone must always be to blame, someone that needs to be sued, slapped, and slandered; but not ourselves. We seek justice for others, and mercy for ourselves. Fixing blame doesn't help resolve the problems of American children or help them to achieve a brighter future. To help them, we've got to get the issues right, which means getting beneath the easy stereotypes that so profoundly influence attitudes toward children at-risk and their families.

The question is, Will we get the issues right? Children do not vote. They do not have organized lobbies and are dependent on others to carry their cause before the nation and before policy makers. In order to get the issues right, teachers must be joined by other Americans of goodwill who possess a large, generous, and forward-looking social vision, to champion children by telling the truth about their plight and by celebrating their goodness and courage. The cause of children, of all causes, ought to galvanize Americans to action. Will we be willing to do what is necessary and right, to invest what is needed, to help these 34 children, all children, to have safer, richer, more interesting and productive lives inside and outside of schools? This is the standard against which America and its leaders must be judged.

Notes

Chapter 1

1. Popenoe, D. (1996). A world without fathers. *The Wilson Quarterly, 20* (2), 15.

2. Cox, H. (March 1999). The market is god. *The Atlantic Monthly, 283*(3), 18–23.

3. An initial set of questions emerged from my general aim to understand more about the children's lives and what they thought about school, what they hoped for themselves and for their families, and what issues concerned them. This initial set of questions was tested with a few children not involved in the study and rewritten in response to their responses. Nevertheless, in many of the interviews I found it necessary to adjust the questions and follow the children's lead. I also found it necessary to vary how I posed the questions because of the age of the children and sometimes because of the nature of my relationship with them. Not all questions were asked in any single interview, and frequently when asked they were stated in a slightly different form. Additionally, sometimes the children would wander around a question rather than answer it directly, and sometimes they would simply say whatever popped into their minds.

The following questions provided the framework for interviewing the children:

> How old are you?
> Do you have brothers or sisters?
> With whom do you live?
> Name the schools you have attended?
> What is your favorite way to spend time?
> When you get home from school, what do you do? (Then what?)
> Do you help with fixing dinner?
> Does your family have rules you must follow? Would you give me an
>   example? What happens when you break a rule?
> Do you have chores? Like what?
> How much T.V. do you watch? Do you have a favorite T.V. program?
> What time do you go to bed?
> What time do you get up in the morning?
> Are you a good student? Are good grades important? What is a good student?

(*Probes*: What does a good student do? What does a poor student do? How does a good student differ from a poor one?)

Do you do homework? Does anyone help you with your homework?

Do you enjoy school? (*Probe*: What do you like best about it?)

What subjects—the things you study in school–do you like best? (*Probe*: What do you like best about it?)

What subjects don't you like? (*Probe*: What don't you like about _____?)

Do you like to read? Do you have a favorite book? Do you have books at home?

Do you like your teachers? Do your teachers like you? How can you tell they like you?

Do your teachers want you to do well in school, to learn?

What do you want to be when you grow up? (When you dream about the future, what do you see yourself doing?) What do you have to do to become a _____?

Do you worry?

When you feel sad, what do you do?

Do other kids like you?

Do you have a best friend? What do you like to do with that friend? What does that friend like about you?

When something good happens to you, why does it happen?

When something bad happens to you, why does it happen?

This is a genie question. Do you know what a genie is? Imagine I'm a genie who can do anything, change anything, make anything happen. I say to you, you can have one wish—but you must wish for whatever it is that will make you most happy. What would you have me do, or change? (*Note*: Some children prefer a direct question, so ask: "What in all the world would make you most happy?")

Same question with a school focus: Imagine I'm a genie again, and I say to you, you can have one wish but this time you must wish for the one thing or change that would make you happier when you are in school. What would you have me do?

Do you have any questions for me?

Parental interviews were organized around these questions:

Tell me about _____.

Is your child a good student? (If not, what would improve the situation?)

What do you see your child doing in the future, 5, 10 years?

If you had the power to make one thing happen or to change one thing for your child, what would it be?

When you think of your child, do you have any concerns or worries?

In addition, questions were sometimes asked to clarify or check something a child said in the interview.

Teachers were asked the following:

Characterize _____.
Do you know his or her family?
What kind of year has _____ had in school?
Do you have any concerns for his or her future?
What would you hope for him or her?
If you could do one thing to help _____ what would it be?
What advice would you give to his or her teacher next year?

4. Guba, E. (1978). *Toward a methodology of naturalistic inquiry in educational evaluation.* Los Angeles: Center for the Study of Evaluation, UCLA Graduate School of Education, p. 53.

5. See, for example, Rosenthal, B. S. (1998). Non-school correlates of dropout: An integrative review of the literature. *Children and Youth Services Review, 20*(5), 413–433. Even such seemingly simple issues as why young people leave school reveal the incredible difficulty of separating variables in order to establish causal relationships.

6. Kegan, R. (1982). *The evolving self: Problem and process in human development.* Cambridge: Harvard University Press.

Chapter 2

1. Brooks-Gunn, J. & Duncan, G. J. (1997). The effects of poverty on children. *Children and Poverty, 7*(2), 55.

2. These figures come from a variety of sources. See, "Children '99: Countdown to the Millennium Fact Sheet," Child Welfare League of America. Statistics are available on the Internet (www.cwla.org) from the Child Welfare League of America by state under the categories of child abuse and neglect, child health, child care and education, violence, and income support. The figures are updated yearly. The state figures are taken from the 1998 and 1999 reports.

3. *Ibid*, p. 57.

4. Child Welfare League of America. (1998). Children '98: America's promise fact sheet. Author, 1.

5. For helpful discussions of attention deficit disorders and their treatment, see Hallowell, E. M. & Ratey, J. J. (1994). *Driven to distraction: Recognizing and coping with attention deficit disorder from childhood through adulthood.* New York: Simon and Schuster. See also, Garber, S. W., Garber, M. D. & Spizman, R. F. (1996). *Beyond ritalin.* New York: Villard Books.

6. Child Welfare League of America. (1999). Children '99: Countdown to the millennium fact sheet. Author, 1.

7. Liederman, D. S. (1999). Amendment to housing bill would leave a million children homeless. Child Welfare League of America.

8. Child Welfare League of America. (1997). Quality child care makes a difference. Author. See also Brooks-Gunn, J. & Duncan, G. J. (1997). The effects of poverty on children. *Children and Poverty, 7*(2), 55–71.

9. Slavin, R. E., Karweit, N. L. & Wasik, B. A. (1992). *Preventing early school failure: What works?* Baltimore, MD: The Johns Hopkins University, Center for Research on Effective Schooling for Disadvantaged Students.

Chapter 3

1. Dreman, S., Spielberger, C. & Fried, R. (1999). The experience and expression of anger in divorced mothers: Effects on behavior problems in children. *Journal of Divorce & Remarriage, 30*(3/4), 39.

2. See Grych, J. H. & Fincham, F. D. (1992). Interventions for children of divorce: Toward greater integration of research and action. *Psychological Bulletin, 111*(3), 434–455.

3. See Rotenberg, K. J., Kim, L. S. & Herman-Stahl, M. (1998). *Journal of Divorce & Remarriage, 29*(1/2), 43–66.

4. See Jeynes, W. H. (1998). Does divorce or remarriage have the greater negative impact on the academic achievement of children? *Journal of Divorce & Remarriage, 29*(1/2), 79–101.

5. Children are often profoundly upset by having to share their mother when she dates. They tend to be jealous of the time the parent spends away from home when dating. In addition, there appears to be a perception on the part of the child of increasing loss of control. A child may respond to these feelings with increased aggression. Moreover, it is very difficult for the parent and child to discuss the topic of dating in ways the child will understand. See Sumner, W. C. (1997). The effects of parental dating on latency children living with one custodial parent. *Journal of Divorce & Remarriage, 27*(1/2), 137–157.

6. High anxiety of the type Zeke manifested is associated with low coping skills. *Ibid*, p. 62.

7. Sumner (1997).

8. In many respects, Little Dan is a miracle child. Fetal alcohol syndrome (FAS) is now the leading cause of mental retardation in the Western world. The fact that Little Dan is the sole focus of his grandparents' attention provides hope that he will do much better than expected in his intellectual development. Like other children with FAS, fully 85 percent, he suffers from hyperactivity and is impulsive, has difficulty concentrating, and struggles when processing information. See Phelps, L. (1995). Psychoeducational outcomes of fetal alcohol syndrome. *School Psychology Review, 24*(2), 200–212.

9. See Brooks, D. & Barth, R. P. (1998). Characteristics and outcomes of drug-exposed and non drug-exposed children in kinship and non-relative foster care. *Children and Youth Services Review, 20*(6), 475–501.

10. Popenoe, D. (1996). A world without fathers. *Wilson Quarterly, 20*(2), 12–29.

11. The struggle in America over the place of men in the family has gone through a number of stages. Perhaps intended to comfort and strengthen mothers left on their own to raise children, the view that men don't matter has likely had the unintended consequence of marginalizing men, of excusing and then easing

their path away from familial responsibility. Some circles are vicious, and especially this one. Consider: on the whole, children in two-parent families not only do better in school but also are better socially adjusted and better able to successfully cope with problems, especially disappointment. All one needs to do is visit American prisons to have this conclusion brought forcefully home. Fully three fourths of inmates grew up without a father, and the vast majority of inmates are, of course, male, over 90 percent; lacking boundaries established and sustained by fathers, boys find gangs, boys pretending to be men. All told, about 30 percent of children of divorce get caught up in a pattern of troubling behavior. Boys externalize and act out, while girls often quietly internalize problems. Boys who are young when their parents divorce, and who display behavior problems, are likely to continue acting out through adolescence. Sixty percent of America's rapists and over 70 percent of its adolescent murderers are from fatherless homes. Both boys and girls often disengage from the family; they also tend to disengage from school: Children from disrupted families are about twice as likely to drop out of high school as other children. See, Rosenthal B. S. (1998). Non-school correlates of dropout: An integrative review of the literature. *Children and Youth Services Review, 20*(5), 411–433.

12. For a discussion of these points, see Gutmann, D. (1998). The paternal imperative. *The American Scholar, 67*(1), 118–126.

13. Men outside of the family also can help. There is a desperate need for more male elementary school teachers and for more school-based programs for children that involve men in mentoring roles with both boys and girls. Sadly, this need has received virtually no attention in policy debates nationally. Lafayette is unusual in that there are two men on faculty. Big brother and big sister programs, along with scouting, make a positive difference for children.

The task before us reaches well beyond the schools and voluntary programs that are currently available to help children, however. A national effort is required, and a fundamental cultural shift toward supporting marriage and encouraging disengaged men to turn their hearts toward their children.

Chapter 4

1. Additionally, 6 percent of women entering prison are pregnant. See Child Welfare League of America. (1998). *Children with parents in prison: Child welfare policy, program and practice issues.* Author. www.cwla.org.

2. Child Welfare League of America. (February 1997). *Child Welfare League of America's alcohol and other drug survey of state child welfare agencies.* Author. www.cwla.org.

3. Josiah is like many children with parents who abuse illegal drugs: Among other negative effects on children, chemical abuse at home leads to children who have "low self-esteem, feel responsible for their parents' behavior, and have an inaccurate self-perception." Feaster, C. B. (1996). The relationship between parental chemical abuse and children's behavior disorders. *Preventing School Failure, 40*(4), 155–160.

4. See, Rodgers-Farmer, A. Y. (1999). Parenting stress, depression, and parenting in grandmothers raising their grandchildren. *Children and Youth Service Review, 21*(5), 377–388.

5. See Feaster (1996).

6. Child Welfare League of America. (n.d.). The relationship between chemical dependency and the child welfare system. Author. www.cwla.org.

7. Child Welfare League of America. (1997). "It is estimated that currently 50% to 80% of children who enter the child welfare system do so because of familial substance abuse."

8. Dore, M. M. (1999). Emotionally and behaviorally disturbed children in the welfare system: Points of preventive intervention. *Children and Youth Services Review, 21*(1), 7–29.

9. Child Welfare League of America. (October 1997). *CWLA testimony to the Ways and Means Subcommittee on Human Resources for hearing on parental substance abuse and child abuse.* Author. www.cwla.org.

Chapter 5

1. There is a lively and intense debate currently raging over issues related to child abuse. Interpretations even vary regarding how serious the problem is. See *Child sexual abuse.* (1998). San Diego: Greenhaven Press. Similar debates rage over issues of family violence. See *Family violence.* (1996). San Diego: Greenhaven Press.

2. The National Family Violence Surveys have prompted much debate. One surprising outcome was that "women in the two national surveys had a high rate of assault on their spouses and indeed often hit first . . . whereas studies of women in shelters show that they almost never assault their partner." Straus, M. A. (1990). Injury and frequency of assault and the "representative sample fallacy" in measuring wife beating and child abuse. In M. S. Straus & R. J. Gelles (Eds.), *Physical violence in American families* (pp. 75–89). New Brunswick, NJ: Transaction Publishers. Moreover, women appear to be about as violent as men: "We found that among couples where violence occurred, both partners are violent in about half of the cases, violence by only the male partner occurs one-quarter of the time, and violence by only the female partner occurs one-quarter of the time . . . [W]e find that women initiate violence about as often as men." Stets, J. E. & Straus, J. A. (1990). Gender differences in reporting marital violence and its medical and psychological consequences. In M. S. Straus & R. J. Gelles (Eds.), *Physical violence in American families* (pp. 151–165). New Brunswick, NJ: Transaction Publishers.

3. See U.S. Department of Health and Human Services. (1998). *Child maltreatment 1996: Reports from the states to the National Child Abuse and Neglect Data System.* Washington, DC: U.S. Government Printing Office.

4. Child Welfare League of America. (September 1998). Juvenile Justice Policy Network. Author.

5. See Gelles, R. J. & Straus, M. A. (1988). *Intimate violence.* New York: Simon and Schuster, 109–113.

6. Salzinger, S., Feldman, R. S., Hammer, M. & Rosario, M. (1993). The effects of physical abuse on children's social relationships. *Child Development, 64*, 182.

7. Eisikovits, Z., Winstok, Z. & Enosh, G. (1998). Children's experience of interparental violence: A heuristic model. *Children and Youth Services Review, 20*(6), 562–563.

8. Rowe, E. & Eckenrode, J. (1999). The timing of academic difficulties among maltreated and nonmaltreated children. *Child Abuse and Neglect, 23*(8), 813–832. See also Leiter, J. & Johnsen, M. C. (1997). Child maltreatment and school performance declines: An event-history analysis. *American Educational Research Journal, 34*(3), 563–589.

9. Waldron, N. L. (1996). Child abuse and disability: The school's role in prevention and intervention. *Preventing School Failure, 40*(4), 166.

10. The following "signs" of maltreatment are ones teachers and other caregivers should be aware of:

Signs of neglect. Lack of adequate food, clothing, and/or housing; poor hygiene; thin, emaciated, distended stomach; needs medical, dental, and/or psychiatric care; lack of supervision or guidance; given inappropriate food, drink, or drugs; abandonment. Children facing these problems often demonstrate the following behavior: self-destructive; depressed, dull, apathetic appearance; food-associated problems (begs, steals, refuses to eat); extremes at school (frequently absent or tardy, constant fatigue or listlessness, falls asleep in class); developmental lags; reports that no caretaker is at home. When meeting the child's caretakers they may seem apathetic or passive, depressed, socially isolated and little concerned about the child. Such people may not respond to inquiries.

Signs of physical abuse. The child shows unexplained injuries of various kinds (bruises, welts, burns, fractures, cuts); absences correlate with injury. In class the child might be overly compliant, passive, withdrawn, undemanding, or aggressive, easily frightened, fearful; wary of physical contact or touch; have difficulty positively interacting with other children; be afraid to go home; destructive to self and/or others; runs away; complains of soreness or moves uncomfortably; wears clothing inappropriate to weather conditions, or to cover the body. The caretaker may conceal the child's injury and seem unconcerned; describe the child as bad, different, selfish; believe in severe discipline; have unrealistic expectations; abuse alcohol or drugs; be markedly immature; and project blame on others.

Emotional abuse. The child might have a range of physical problems (exacerbated by emotional distress, speech disorders, delayed physical development, ulcers, allergies). In school the child might behave in extreme ways (overly passive or complaint, aggressive or demanding); demonstrate overly adaptive behavior (inappropriately mature, inappropriately infantile); show developmental lags (mental, emotional) and signs of long-term depression. Sleep disorders might be present as well as conduct disorders (anti-social, destructive, delinquent behavior) and habit disorders (sucking, rocking, biting). The caretaker may have unrealistic expectations of child; may threaten the child and engage in name-calling or belittling; may treat siblings unequally; may withhold love and show little concern.

Sexual abuse. Teachers may notice torn, stained, or bloody underclothing; difficulty walking or sitting; bruises, blood from body cavities; a loss of appetite;

unexplained gagging; excessive pain or itching in genital area; and frequent unexplained sore throats. Sexually abused children may withdraw, become clinging, whiny, hysterical, showing a lack of emotional control. They may cry without reason. Some run away. Unusually infantile behavior and bizarre behavior may be demonstrated, along with sophisticated or unusual sexual behavior or knowledge. Other signs include fear of physical contact, of closeness, eating disorders, avoidance of bathrooms, sudden difficulties in school, role reversal and being overly concerned for siblings.

These are among the many signs of potential abuse, signs that prompted concern for Chuck and for Marshall. Teachers have a legal and moral obligation to take action when signs of abuse are recognized. Procedures for taking action are clear and widely available and teachers need to know them. From Utah State Division of Family Services. (1993). *Child abuse and neglect protocol: Policies and procedures for the handling of suspected child abuse cases for school personnel, child protective services and law enforcement.* Salt Lake City, UT: Author.

Chapter 6

1. Gilbert, K. R. (1996). "We've had the same loss, why don't we have the same grief?" Loss and differential grief in families. *Death Studies, 20,* 269–283.

2. See Worden, J. W. & Silverman, P. R. (1996). Parental death and the adjustment of school-age children. *Omega, 33*(2), 91–102.

3. "Using the surviving parent's report, [it was found] that bereaved children, when assessed one month after the death, showed more depressed mood and deterioration of school performance than did the controls. By thirteen months bereaved children showed a decrease in depressive mood but also showed a significant increase in abdominal pain, conflict with siblings, and disinterest in school." *Ibid,* p. 92.

4. A lively spiritual life can have a profound and positive effect on children's struggle to make sense of life following a disaster. See Coles, R. (1990). *The spiritual life of children.* Boston: Houghton Mifflin.

5. This is a very common fear, perhaps experienced by most children who suffer the loss of a parent. See Sandler, I., Gersten, J., Reynolds, K., Kallgren, C. & Ramirez, R. (1988). Using theory and data to plan support interventions. In B. Gottlieb (ed.), *Marshalling social support,* pp. 53–83. Newbury Park, CA: Sage Publications.

6. Wessel, M. A. (1984). Thoughts of a pediatrician. In H. Wass & C. A. Corr (Eds.), *Childhood and death* (p. 212). Washington, DC: Hemisphere Publishing Corporation.

7. Furman, E. (1984). Children's patterns in mourning the death of a loved one. In H. Wass & C. A. Corr (Eds.), *Childhood and death* (pp. 185–203). Washington, DC: Hemisphere Publishing Corporation.

8. Worden and Silberman (1996).

9. Wessel (1996), pp. 212–213.

10. Worden, J. W. (1996). *Children and grief: When a parent dies* (pp. 12–16). New York: The Guilford Press.

11. Mahon, M. M., Goldberg, R. L. & Washington, S. K. (1999). Discussing death in the classroom: Beliefs and experiences of educators and education students. *Omega, 39*(2), 99–121.

Chapter 7

1. Brad's stepmother's feelings are not unusual, although Brad's problems present especially difficult challenges. "One of the most stressful aspects of being a stepmother is learning to focus less on the stepchildren. Since most women want their stepchildren to like them, they often start out focusing too much on what the children want and too little on what the adults and the marriage need." Nielsen, L. (1999). Stepmothers: Why so much stress? A review of the research. *Journal of Divorce & Remarriage, 30*(1/2), 134.
2. Erikson, E. H. (1963). *Childhood and society.* New York: W. W. Norton.

Chapter 8

1. Lasch, C. (1991). *The true and only heaven: Progress and its critics.* New York: W. W. Norton, 81.
2. See Dore, M. M. (1999). Emotionally and behaviorally disturbed children in the child welfare system: Points of preventative intervention. *Children and Youth Services, 21*(1), 7–29.

Chapter 9

1. Haberman, M. (1995). *Star teachers of children in poverty.* West Lafayette, IN: Kappa Delta Pi, 32.
2. Haberman, M. (1991). The pedagogy of poverty versus good teaching. *Phi Delta Kappan,* December, 290–294.
3. Tyack, D. & Cuban, L. (1995). *Tinkering toward Utopia: A century of public school reform.* Cambridge: Harvard University Press.
4. See Knapp, M. S., Shields, P. M. & Turnbull, B. J. (1995). Academic challenge in high-poverty classrooms. *Phi Delta Kappan,* June, 770–776.
5. National Commission on Teaching and America's Future. (1996). *What matters most: Teaching for America's future.* New York: Author.
6. Slavin, R. E., Karweit, N. L. & Wasik, B. A. (1992). *Preventing early school failure: What works?* Baltimore: The Johns Hopkins University, Center for Research on Effective Schooling for Disadvantaged Students.
7. See, Rose, L. C. & Gallup, A. M. (September 2000). The 32nd annual Phi Delta Kappa/Gallup poll of the public's attitudes toward the public schools. *Phi Delta Kappan,* 41–57.
8. Sparks, D. & Hirsh, S. (2000). Strengthening professional development: A national strategy. *Education Week, XIX*(37), 42.
9. "America continues to be the world's biggest education spender, but precollegiate teachers here may not be getting their fair share. . . . The United States

spends almost twice as much per college student than the average industrialized country, and its per pupil spending in secondary schools is outpaced by only two of the 27 countries that are part of the Organization for Economic Co-operation and Development. But U.S. teachers' salaries are just slightly higher than the OECD average, and rank low when compared with those of other U.S. college-educated workers in the United States. . . . " Hoff, D. J. (2000). International report finds U.S. teacher salaries lagging. *Education Week, XIX*(36), 5.

    10. Sandham, J. L. (2000). Calif. schools get rankings based on tests. *Education Week, XIX*(21), 16. See also Bowman, D. H. (2000). New York adopts plan for rating all schools based on test scores. *Education Week, XIX*(36), 23.

    11. Sack, J. L. (2000). Del. ties school job reviews to student tests. *Education Week, XIX*(34), 24.

    12. Viadero, D. (2000). Lags in minority achievement defy traditional explanations. *Education Week, XIX*(28), 19.

    13. Bullough, R. V., Jr. (1988). *The forgotten dream of American public education.* Ames: Iowa State University Press.

    14. When thinking through this section of the chapter I drew on work by Ann S. Masten. See Masten, A. S. (1994). "Resilience in individual development: Successful adaptation despite risk and adversity" in M. C. Wang & E. W. Gordon (Eds.), *Educational resilience in inner-city America: Challenges and prospects* (pp. 3–25). Hillsdale, NJ: Lawrence Erlbaum. See also Pasternack, R. & Martinez, K. (1996). Resiliency: What is it and how can correctional educational practices encourage its development? *Preventing School Failure, 40*(2), 63–66.

    15. Miller, D. (1997). Mentoring structures: Building a protective community. *Preventing School Failure, 41*(3), 107. See also Guetzloe, E. (1997). The power of positive relationships: Mentoring programs in school and community. *Presenting School Failure, 41*(3), 100–104.

    16. Bradley, A. (2000). Study finds positive effects from Minn. welfare policies. *Education Week, XIX*(39), 18.

Index

About the Author

Robert V. Bullough, Jr. is Professor of Teacher Education and a researcher within CITIES, the Center for the Improvement of Teacher Education and Schooling, Brigham Young University, Provo, Utah. He is also Emeritus Professor of Educational Studies, University of Utah. Author of numerous publications on education and teaching, his greatest accomplishment is raising, with his wife, Dawn Ann, four children who are turning out to be good people.